∜ **W9-BWN-647**

**THIS BOOK IS DEDICATED
TO
THE BELOVED CONGREGATION
OF
THE FIRST BAPTIST CHURCH
IN NEWTON, MASSACHUSETTS**

*We are bound to give thanks to God always
for you . . . as is fitting, because your faith is
growing abundantly, and the love of every
one of you for one another is increasing.*

2 Thessalonians 1:3

Postscript to Preaching

After forty years, how will I preach today?

Gene E. Bartlett

Judson Press ® Valley Forge

Postscript to Preaching

Copyright © 1981
Judson Press, Valley Forge, PA 19481

All rights reserved. No part of this publication may be reproduced, stored in a retrieval
system, or transmitted in any form or by any means, electronic, mechanical, photocopying,
recording, or otherwise, without the prior permission of the copyright owner, except for
brief quotations included in a review of the book.

Unless otherwise indicated, Bible quotations in this volume are from the Revised Standard
Version of the Bible, copyrighted 1946, 1952, 1971, 1973 © by the Division of Christian
Education of the National Council of the Churches of Christ in the United States of America,
and are used by permission.

Other versions of the Bible quoted in this book are:

The *New American Standard Bible,* © The Lockman Foundation 1960, 1962, 1963, 1968, 1971,
1972, 1973, 1975. Used by permission.

The Holy Bible, King James Version

The Bible: A New Translation by James Moffatt. Copyright 1954 by James Moffatt. Reprinted
by permission of Harper & Row, Publishers, Inc.

Library of Congress Cataloging in Publication Data
  Bartlett, Gene E.
    Postscript to preaching.
    Includes bibliographical references.
    1. Pastoral theology.   2. Preaching.   I. Title.
    BV4011.B373   253   80-24394
    ISBN 0-8170-0909-4

The name JUDSON PRESS is registered as a trademark in the U.S. Patent Office. Printed
in the U.S.A.

Contents

Introduction

In my senior year at college I was invited to speak in the village church on "What I Expect to Find in the Ministry." Recently I came upon that manuscript, now embarrassingly brittle and yellowed with age, waiting like a kind of Dead Sea Scroll for my rediscovery! Reading it brought a few nostalgic moments as I looked back on that young man about to begin a ministry, looking forward with untested anticipation to it. It reminded me that we can become strangers to ourselves—until reintroduced.

What about those expectations with which I approached the ministry? In the senior years of my life a counterpart question appears: Did I actually find what I expected?

I have to say with some sense of wonder that the answer is yes. Most of those things mentioned in that talk of many years ago were indeed found in the living of the years: the close engagement with people at the primary human experiences of their lives, the excitement of trying to interpret the biblical faith in a constantly changing situation, the loving relation to a congregation, the trust relationship with persons in their times of celebration or deep trouble, the satisfaction of a lifetime of study, the confrontation with the social issues of the time.

Of course there were also the realities which mark any human experience. There were the times of spiritual dryness when I received only "dusty answers" in my search for certainty. There were the times of persistent intellectual questioning when I understood all too well the confession of Wordsworth after the French Revolution:

> I lost
> All feeling of conviction, and, in fine,
> Sick, wearied out with contrarieties,
> Yielded up moral questions in despair. . . .[1]

There were the times when, faced by overwhelming social problems, I wondered what to advocate and, if I advocated it, whether my action would "do any good." There was the constantly recurring feeling that when I had done my best, I was "not getting it across." Yet with all these times, there never was the feeling that I could do anything else. There was no option but to see it through to the end.

Unexpected Realities

But even a cursory review of these four decades of ministry brings another truth to the fore. What is even more impressive has been the appearance of realities which were not expected. I suspect that even the most prophetic among us did not foresee that these four decades were to bring changes in human life probably more profound and far-reaching than any similar span of time in history. Every generation probably feels that way about itself. But when I consider the movement from the Great Depression to the nuclear and space age, and when I consider further that by the communications revolution changes come to the whole world at once, I believe there is a good case for calling these four decades unparalleled.

There seem to me to be two marks of those changes as we have experienced them, not only in the idea-realm but in the life-realm.

The first is upheaval. We anticipated—and welcomed—change. We felt it necessary, even imperative. But generally we thought of it in evolutionary terms. In fact, the whole concept of evolution, the acceptance of which in itself was a hard-fought battle, at last had moved into our thinking about life in most of its aspects.

But just when that concept had become established, the changes began to come, not by evolution, but by revolution. The words were crisis, upheaval, overthrow, turmoil. Politically, one-half of the world's people have undergone revolution of some kind in these years, one-third of them since World War II.[2] In scientific thinking, in sexual morality, in communication and transportation, in racial relationships, in what we expect from life, there have been radical changes, some for the better, some for the worse, but change. Often that change came as upheaval, wave after wave of upheaval.

The second mark, even more significant, is the rise of the secular. It is indeed the spirit of this age, dominating almost every aspect of life. It has moved from being a process called secularization to being a profession of faith called secularism.

Politically emerging states are *avowedly* secular. Secularism has become the established religion of vast modern states, some Communist, some Socialist, some "secular democracies." The secular view of life has become the basis for their behavior and the ordering of their societies. It seems not only stated, but also required.

In morality, secularism has produced a remarkable pluralism. The question asked is not "What does the Lord require of me?" but "What does my chosen life-style require?" Morality is almost completely secular, often pragmatic, usually peer-oriented, and generally "for the time being."

The literature of our time again and again not only reflects secularism but also preaches it. The dominant voices support John Fowles's assertion in *The French Lieutenant's Woman:*

> The river of life, of mysterious laws and mysterious choice, flows past a deserted embankment . . . life . . . is not a symbol, is not one riddle and one failure to guess it, is not to inhabit one face alone or to be given up after one losing throw of the dice; but is to be, however inadequately, emptily, hopelessly into the city's iron heart, endured.[3]

There seems to me no escape from the fact that the voices that describe and therefore interpret our time are overwhelmingly secular.

It was inevitable that the secular should penetrate the church as well, both as a process and, more than we admit, as a faith. Often the model for church organization is the corporation; the church's structures and forms of management reflect the corporation more than the distinctive nature of church life as such. The size and number of our bureaucracies bear testimony to our faith in secular ways of doing things.

Another evidence of the power of secularism is the kind

of "spheres of influence" agreement which seems to have been struck between the church and the areas of our common life. Secularism does not necessarily eliminate or openly oppose the biblical faith. It has a more subtle plan. *It puts it on a reservation* where it has domain, but beyond which it may not go. Generally this attitude can be stated simplistically, as I have heard it stated in Communist countries: "We have no quarrel with the church as long as it sticks to its business." And its business is generally quite otherworldly, thus leaving this world to other authorities.

There have been several diverse reactions to this secularization of life. Many look upon it as a kind of liberation, even the work of God in the world. We have at last been set free, they feel, from the domination of the church over our common life.

Others will insist that these matters are "in the stratosphere" and don't really affect the daily lives of people. This overlooks completely that these are precisely the influences which determine the *climate* of our time, and that climate affects all our common life.

As a personal testimony I can say that in every year of my ministry I have been increasingly aware of the secularization of life in practice, in belief, in morality, in the concept of the good life, and in the sovereignties which govern life. There are times then when one must say, "How shall I sing the Lord's song in a strange land?"

Yet in my more faithful moments, I find excitement in the belief that God is bringing forth fresh understanding of the Word by making us confront the secular. Perhaps *that* is the way God is bringing forth new light from the Word, doing a new thing among us. It has quickened a tremendous curiosity in me, and I wish I could be around to see how it comes out!

Reviewing Assumptions

More immediately, these realities of upheaval and the rise of the secular have forced upon Christian preachers an urgent task. We are called upon to review the main questions we are asking and the main themes we are preaching. This does not necessarily mean that we are questioning their truth (though that cannot be ruled out), but that we *are* questioning our ways of communicating it—the words we use, the human situations we address, the categories of our thought and the very nature of preaching itself. The pages which follow represent one man's grappling with these questions. They are second thoughts that come at this end of ministry.

This material has been rewritten from two sets of lectures which I gave. The first was the Theodore H. Adams Lectures at Southeastern Seminary. The second was the Joseph P. Nordenhaug Lectures at the Baptist Theological Seminary in Ruschlikon, Switzerland. These lectures have been enriched and amplified by the discernment with which they were received and the grace of the hospitality which my wife and I were given. These pages are a modest way of expressing our gratitude to both of these communities.

CHAPTER 1

When Is Preaching Biblical?

To the proposition that preaching ought to be biblical, most of us give ready assent. In fact, too ready! For that has far more radical implications than our easy acceptance suggests. If preaching is really biblical, it stands off against our secular culture in tension at several crucial points.

When *is* preaching biblical? It we take our sermon from words in the Bible, does that in itself make it biblical? Obviously not. It has been said that we preachers have a way of making a peck of our own words from a pint of the Bible's.

Biblical words obviously can be used for nonbiblical purposes. In our time, for example, it is common to use them to support the assumptions of a civil religion. Why is it that the most flagrant forms of civil religion always claim the Bible as their symbol and support? Sometimes those words are used as expressions of a current psychological fad. And they work! It has been said that a well put together unreality is pretty hard to beat. More often than we admit, our biblical words are put to the use of our latest denominational promotional scheme. No doubt about it! Biblical words do not guarantee biblical preaching.

Then what does? Perhaps we shall come to a deeper understanding when we stand before what Karl Barth called "the fundamental alarm." The theological revolution which took place in him began when he faced the question of preaching. It was not, how *do* you preach, but, how *can* you preach?

He faced a question: "What can it mean? It means above all that we should feel a fundamental alarm. What are you doing, you man, with the word of *God* upon *your* lips? Upon what grounds do you assume the rôle of mediator between heaven and earth?"[1]

How can anyone be prepared for real biblical preaching who has not faced that "fundamental alarm"? It is possible that the preacher who stands stammering and overawed by the Word he or she is trying to bring is nearer the truth than the preacher who stands, open book in hand, and glibly proclaims, "The Bible says. . . ." When one further sets that Word against the assumptions of a secular day, both those that are explicit and those that are hidden, it becomes even more overawing. For to preach biblically in a secular day is to engage in a war of the worlds: the biblical world on the one hand, and the secular world on the other. How in the world, then, shall we preach biblically?

It may be helpful for us to divide our thought into two sections. The first considers two principles of biblical interpretation which can be useful to the modern preacher. The second speaks of four basic and radical themes which characterize the biblical witness. These cannot possibly cover a subject so vast, but they can take us two steps on our way!

Two Principles of Interpretation

We turn first then to two principles of interpretation which may be helpful to us. There is first the principle that *in approaching the Bible we are required to define the original meaning of any passage, but not to be confined by it.* The first task of the preacher is to let the Bible speak for itself. But the next task is to let it speak to our time. The first requires scholarship. The second is a task of homiletics. Exegesis must include both; without either it is incomplete. The first without the second leaves one open to the common observation, "That was a good sermon for Paul. Too bad he wasn't here to hear it." The second without the first is rootless and ultimately fruitless, more given to novelty than reality.

When I was a boy in the Ohio valley, I often watched the river boats carrying their cargo up and down the Ohio River. One day it struck me as strange that when they unloaded cargo in my town, they unloaded onto another boat called the wharf boat. Why didn't they build a dock? One day I asked the wharfmaster, and he pointed out what should have been obvious. The level of the stream constantly was changing. If they built a dock, one day it would be too high, another day too low. So they anchored a boat that could rise and fall with the changing levels of the river. He pointed to great chains that ran up the bank to iron stakes. That wharf boat was anchored against the drift of the stream, but free to rise with the changing levels of the river.

That seems to me to be the mark of biblical preaching: anchored against the drift, but afloat on the changing levels of any time. We preachers can err either way. Some of us are anchored but not afloat. Others are afloat but not anchored. Biblical preaching is exciting when it is both.

It may help to take an example. Consider chapter 44 of Isaiah. The prophet makes a telling commentary on the maker of idols. He pictures a man who plants an ash tree, which the rain and the sun cause to grow. When it is mature, he cuts the tree and brings it out of the woods. Then he discovers that he is cold, and he uses the first part of the wood to build a fire to warm himself. In his exertion he has become hungry; so he uses some more of the wood to make a fire to cook his dinner. When he thus is warm and fed, he looks about him and finds that he has some scraps of wood left. At this point Isaiah makes his thrust, for he says with biting caricature, "And the residue thereof he maketh a god . . ." (v. 17, KJV). Isaiah was not here dealing with symbols; he was dealing with the actual practice of his time. He had seen it happen.

But when we have found its truth, how rapidly it illumines *our* generation. It would be difficult to think of a more apt description of secularism than that: warmed first, fed second, and out of the residue we make our gods. Suddenly we find our time illumined, its values set forth, its idolatries exposed. Here we can enter into Isaiah's time and return to our time with a remarkable relevance.

This truth can be summed up in an observation which Dr. Edgar J. Goodspeed once made about the apostle Paul. He said that Paul had a remarkable way of tunneling in on a particular and coming out on a universal. We first must understand and respect the particular. The Bible has a right to speak for itself. But when it comes out on the universal, it is the preacher's task to bring it home to our time, too.

Consider now a second principle of interpretation. *It is*

the truth that for us the event of Jesus Christ illumines the whole of the biblical witness. As the writer of Hebrews put it, "In many and various ways God spoke of old to our fathers by the prophets; but in these last days he has spoken to us by a Son . . ." (Hebrews 1:1-2). And when that happens, we see the whole record in new light. In one sense, Christian preachers work backward in the Bible. We really cannot go back to being B.C. once we have been A.D. To try to read the Old Testament pretending that the New Testament has not come into being would be make-believe, not belief.

I hasten to make clear that in no sense is this putting down the Old Testament witness. To the contrary, it is repossessing it as only a believer in Jesus Christ can. It is that same Old Testament record with its magnificent vision of God which enables us to comprehend at last the consummate event in Jesus Christ. When we speak of "the event of Jesus Christ," we are not speaking of his earthly ministry alone. We are thinking of the centuries-old roots which produced him. When we possess Christ, we possess the prophets, the psalmists, the historians, and especially those towering figures who are our forebears of faith. My point is that we claim them anew in the light of the fulfillment which came to us in Jesus Christ. In this sense, we come to the Bible laying claim upon Paul's word to the Corinthians, ". . . all things are yours; . . . and ye are Christ's . . ." (1 Corinthians 3:21, 23, KJV). For the Christian preacher that is an emancipation proclamation. That is our viewpoint, our point of starting.

Distinctive Themes of Biblical Preaching

Now we turn to some of those distinctive themes which mark genuine biblical preaching. This does not mean that themes of this magnitude will be sermon subjects, for they cannot be encompassed within a single sermon. But they are the ground within which biblical sermons grow, the main vines from which many branches grow. To lose these out of our thinking and our struggle is to lose the characteristics of truly biblical preaching.

In 1917 Karl Barth gave a lecture which proved to be one of the first marks of his shift in position. The title of the lecture was "The Strange New World Within the Bible." The main thesis was that the Bible is "'not the right human thoughts about God but the right divine thoughts about men.'"[2] It is this essential understanding about the Bible that enables us to affirm at least four themes which mark its word to us.

The first, of course, as we have often noted, is that in which we speak of *the mighty acts of God.* One of the distinctions of the Bible is that men and women not only say, "This is the Lord's saying," but also, "This is the Lord's doing." We will speak of what we believe God has done and what it means in terms of the redemption of persons.

Frankly, I am not altogether satisfied with the phrase "God's mighty acts." More significantly, it seems to me, the Bible speaks of the *God who acts mightily.* It is God whom we trust more than any of God's specific acts.

Phillips Brooks spoke of this in one of his sermons more than a hundred years ago. He said, "There is the faith in what God has done, which believes that He can do it again, and there is faith in the God who did it, which believes that He can do whatever else is needed in any day to come."[3] That, it seems to me, is what we mean when we speak of proclaiming the mighty acts of God. It helps us most to know that when we see those acts, we can believe that if God did what was necessary *then,* God will do what is necessary *now.* God is, in short, a God who acts in every generation.

We must not suppose that in depicting the mighty acts of God we always have to paint on a large canvas. There is a pastoral side to those acts, for they speak of hope to the human heart. After all, the greatest of all mighty acts was the resurrection. Yet for Paul that became intensely personal, "that I may know him and the power of his resurrection . . ." (Philippians 3:10). To preach the mighty acts of God often has a pastoral dimension. It is the personal hope that:

> . . . suddenly above a hill,
> A heavenly lamp set on a heavenly sill
> Will shine for you and point the way to go,
> How well I know.
>
> For I have waited through the dark, and I
> Have seen a star rise in the blackest sky
> Repeatedly—it has not failed me yet.
> And I have learned God never will forget
> To light his lamp. If we but wait for it,
> It will be lit.[4]

The second theme which will run all through our biblical preaching is *God's self-disclosure.* It appears in the Bible in an amazing number of variations: the burning bush before Moses; the stony resting place of Jacob which became Bethel, "the house of God"; the still small voice for Elijah; the Lord high and lifted up in the temple for Isaiah. The list is almost endless, a mighty chorus saying one thing: God has chosen self-disclosure!

Of course any disclosure would have to be self-disclosure. Anything else would be exposure. Who could compel God against God's will? Moses learned that in the moving poetic encounter recorded in chapter 33 of Exodus. He had gone out to the tent of meeting outside the camp to negotiate with God. He even had secured God's promise to go with them to the Promised Land, in spite of God's earlier word to the contrary. Made heady by his success, Moses then asked a daring thing, "Show me thy glory." To this God replied, "I will make all my goodness pass before you, and will proclaim before you my name . . . I will be gracious to whom I will be gracious. . . . But you cannot see my face. . . ." Then God offered an amazing option, "There is a place by me where you shall stand upon the rock; and while my glory passes by I will put you in a cleft of the rock, and I will cover you with my hand until I have passed by; then I will take away my hand, and you shall see my back; but my face shall not be seen.'" (See verses 18-23.) That was no mere fantasy, a flight of imagination! That was poetic description of human experience.

But the Bible moves on to the moment of real disclosure. We believe that Moses' petition has been fulfilled for us. It took Jesus Christ to do it. As Paul says, "For it is the God who said, 'Let light shine out of darkness,' who has shone in our hearts to give the light of the knowledge of the glory of God in the face of Christ" (2 Corinthians 4:6). Like a symphonic theme with many variations it will run through our biblical preaching: God's self-disclosure.

The third theme comes primarily from the New Testament, for it speaks of the *new age.* We are indebted to Paul for giving that faith its form and its substance. In Jesus Christ a new age had come. The world never again could go back. Though the world in its external manifestations continued to have the evil, the darkness, the mystery, it could never again exist in the same way, because a new age had begun. That light was now shining in the midst of the darkness. The first rays of dawn could be seen on the horizon.

If you were to go out tonight a little before midnight and, seeing the darkness, ask what time it is, I would have to answer, "It's night. It's still P.M." The world is still moving into darkness. If, a few moments later, you were to go out and, seeing the same darkness, should ask what time it is, I would have to reply, "It's morning. It's A.M." How can this be? The darkness is the same; the cold is still upon us; there is no outward change, no light on the horizon. But it is a profound change when you go from P.M. to A.M. A new day has begun. The sun has moved to its lowest level and already has started the ascent toward noon. The whole world moves toward morning. It is A.M.

We believe that is the biblical hope which has come to us in Jesus Christ. Ever since his coming, the world has been at A.M. Oh, the darkness is deep, and the cold is still upon us, and the signs of morning are few. But no doubt about it. It is A.M.! The whole world moves toward that day of hope, toward that high noon, which is the Christian vision. Because it is A.M., one change already has come—that in our hearts! We lift up our hearts now because we believe we move toward morning. There is hope *now* because the deepest point has been passed. In a sense we possess morning *now*, in our hearts and minds! We can celebrate its coming.

What an audacious belief that is! But you cannot sit down before the Bible with an open mind without coming to that faith. It proclaims a new age. In Jesus Christ the world went from P.M. to A.M.

The fourth theme that marks biblical preaching is the understanding that we proclaim a *word which requires us to say yes or no*. ". . . I have set before you life and death . . . therefore choose life . . . "(Deuteronomy 30:19). In times of testing we often ask what God is doing and whether God really *is* at work as we have claimed. The answer well may be that God is doing something by confronting us with a choice.

That's true in our personal lives. Erik Erikson has pointed out that in each stage of the life cycle, there always is a positive and a negative.[5] God is saying at every stage, "Choose life." I believe that also is true in history. God *is* lord of history in that God confronts us with choice and keeps options open. One cannot conceive of biblical preaching that does not sound that theme: Choose life.

Yet when we are asked for credentials to proclaim such

a thing, we realize how vulnerable the preacher really is, especially in the contemporary world. It is an exceedingly exposed position. There's no hiding place for the preacher who proclaims the biblical faith. You cannot hide behind a wall of proof, for there is none. You cannot disappear very long into a cloud of sentimentality because people soon see through it—and should. You cannot cover yourself with the claim that, after all, you are such a good person and people love you so much. There are some times when you simply have to say, as Luther did, "'My conscience is thirled to the word of God, and it is neither safe nor honest to act against one's conscience.'"[6]

Yes, there is a vulnerability in the preacher of the Word who has to trust it in the face of besetting doubts and disturbing defeats. Because that vulnerability hurts so much, some of us, like David, try to put on another's armor. That's one of the most humorous pictures in the Bible: The king's armor on a shepherd boy! One can hear them now, putting it on with much clanging and saying, "All right, boy, go get him." The record simply says that David could not move. But he took off the armor and found a few stones for his sling and went out almost totally vulnerable—to take the victory. To find the Word that you can trust courageously is to find the few stones for your sling. It doesn't take away your vulnerability, but it brings some surprising victories. It's a kind of heady and sometimes hilarious way to live!

Transmitting the Truth

In his book *The Eighth Day,* Thornton Wilder causes one of the characters, the Archbishop, to relate a story to give courage to his friend, Frazier. He says that a number of years before, in one of the southern provinces of China, there had been a wave of hatred against all foreigners. In that wave all the members of one of the Catholic missions had been taken prisoner, including a bishop, four priests, and six sisters, all of whom spoke German. "Each [of them] was placed in a small cell in a long, low building made of clay and pebbles." The Archbishop was in the center of the row, the four priests on one side of him and the six nuns on the other, each in a separate cell. There was supposed to be no communication between them. But the Archbishop devised a scheme. He numbered the letters of the alphabet and by tapping on the wall began to communicate with them in a kind of homemade Morse code. When he repeated it often enough, the others picked up the code. By this method the Archbishop sent out words of hope and courage, sustaining their spirits through the dark times. His tapping, of course, could be heard only by the one next to his cell. That person, in turn, had to transmit the same sounds to the opposite wall, and thus it passed down the row.

After some time one of their number died and into that cell went a Portuguese who spoke no German. Hearing the tapping on the wall, he sensed that it was important; so he began to pass it over to the opposite wall to keep the message going down the line. He never really knew what he was communicating, but he sensed it was important to his fellow prisoners, perhaps some plan for escape.

Commenting upon this, the Archbishop felt that in the Portuguese prisoner he saw ourselves at many times in our lives. He concludes, "'Life is surrounded by mysteries beyond the comprehension of our limited minds . . . you and I have seen them. We transmit (we hope) fairer things than we can fully grasp.'"[7]

When we have done our best to understand this amazing biblical word, we still must confess, "We transmit fairer things than we can fully grasp." But only through those who are faithful can the Word of life go out to a world often imprisoned by the tyrannies of the human condition.

CHAPTER 2

Is a Prophetic Ministry Possible Today?

In his book, *Men Who Made the Nation,* John Dos Passos speaks of the role Alexander Hamilton played in the Constitutional Convention. He had come with a plan for the nation. But as time went on, it was evident that it would not be accepted. Finally Hamilton picked up his papers and went home. Commenting upon this, one of the delegates, Dr. Johnson, a college professor from Connecticut, noted, "'Although he has been praised by everybody he has been supported by none.'"[1]

These words about a politician seem to express even more the plight of the prophet in almost every age. The title has carried with it a certain aura, a prestige. Our time is no exception in this regard. Somewhere in its publicity, a seminary tries to slip into its literature the suggestion that it is a "school of the prophets." Most of us, on a more personal scale, hope that when the occasion arises, we will have the courage to show certain prophetic strengths. We count it a compliment when someone observes that *any* utterance we have made is really prophetic! But such words are superficial. They do not guarantee an adequate prophetic ministry for our time. We too can be "praised by everybody but supported by none."

What is the role of the prophet in a secular day? More searchingly, in such a culture is a prophetic ministry really possible? Or have the foundations upon which the prophetic claim rests been so severely eroded that we have no place to stand?

A Biblical Episode

It may be helpful to recall an episode in chapter 18 of Judges. It is recorded that the tribe of Dan had been left out when land had been assigned. But they, too, needed their place in the sun. So they did what any self-respecting tribe would do; they appointed a committee! Five were selected to investigate possibilities. So the five started out to look for available and favorable land. In their travels they came to the hill country of Ephraim and stayed in the home of one Micah. Here they made an amazing discovery. Micah had a priest of his own (the ultimate in status symbols!). Moreover, the priest was a fully pedigreed Levite who had an ephod, the teraphim, a molten and a graven image—all the official paraphernalia of his office. The five decided to consult this priest to see what their prospects for success were. When the priest did his thing and gave a prognosis favorable to the men and their mission, they concluded that he was indeed a true prophet.

Greatly heartened, they went on their way and came to the area of Laish, a land of abundance and prosperity. Best of all, it was a land which had no protective alliances with anyone who would protect it!

So back to the tribe the five went to bring this favorable report and to recommend that the tribe go up and take the land. This time it was not five but six hundred armed men who went to Laish. On the way they came again to the hill country of Ephraim and to the home of Micah. Here the five said to the six hundred, "'Do you know that in these houses there are an ephod, teraphim, a graven image, and a molten image? Now therefore consider what you will do'" (v. 14). This suggestion brought on an immediate, spontaneous "column right," and the six hundred armed men drew up at the gate of Micah's house. The original five went inside to take the ephod, the teraphim, the molten image, and the graven image. At this point the priest came in and said appropriately, "'What are you doing?'" (v. 18). And here is where he got his counsel. They said to him, "'Keep quiet, put your hand upon your mouth, and come with us, and be to us a father and a priest.'" Then they added the clincher. "'Is it better for you to be priest to the house of one man or to be a priest to a whole tribe . . .?'" (v. 19). At this suggestion the priest's ego went on full alert. He entered into a season of decision, about fifteen seconds; and as the story ends, he was seen marching off into the sunset in the midst of the people, carrying his ephod, the teraphim, the molten image, and the graven image. And the record says, "And the priest's heart was glad . . ." (v. 20).

"Keep quiet, put your hand upon your mouth, and come with us, and be to us a father and a priest." The subtle part of that request is that the compromise is not with an evil but with an incomplete good. It is a calling of immense dignity to be father and priest. But can it be the *full* ministry if one accepts the condition, "Keep quiet, put your hand upon your mouth, and come with us"? Is *that* the compromise offered the preacher by a secular day?

The Prophetic Themes

Now let's go back and look at the Old Testament prophets. Consider the context in which they spoke their word. When the Old Testament prophets said, "Thus saith the Lord," they were standing at the center of authority. Around that whole concept the power structure of the nation had been erected. Their voices were the voices of a theocracy. They were calling people to the covenant upon which the nation was founded. As we might claim the authority of the Constitution, the biblical prophets claimed the authority of the covenant. To be sure, the prophets brought their own sensitivity, their enthusiasm, even their ecstasy, to the meaning of that covenant. As John Paterson has said, "They were 'men of the secret' who saw human life in the light of God and spoke of great things yet to come." [2] And when they spoke of them, they had the sanction of the central authority of their culture, an authority which apparently was largely unquestioned.

The amazing stature of these prophets is seen in the fact that they turned that powerful authority to ethical ends. How easy it would have been to turn it to privilege and prerogative! To the contrary! Professor James Muilenburg pointed out that the prophets had five major areas which they constantly addressed:

1. They were concerned for the whole structure of political life in Israel.

2. They had a sharp concern for economic justice.

3. They reminded the nation of the stewardship of the land.

4. They were vigilant about the administration of justice.

5. They had a deep distrust of power.[3]

It would be difficult to think of any concerns more contemporary. In their *theocratic* culture they addressed themselves to those prophetic concerns which must be noted in our *secular* culture. But the prophets spoke from the center of a commonly acknowledged authority: "Thus saith the Lord."

The Secular Contrast

But consider the secular culture in which *we* must carry out the prophetic ministry. The leap from a theocracy to a secular culture is mind-boggling! For over 450 years we have been dividing authority into provinces. Today there are many indeed: the state, the sciences, the arts, corporations, and even the claim of alternate life-styles. Before that pantheon of gods how shall the prophets say, "Thus saith the Lord"? Modern persons could reply, "*Which* Lord?"

Add to this the incredible mixture of cultures and communities. The biblical prophet could speak grandly of "from Dan to Beersheba." Some of us began our ministry when we spoke expansively of "from coast to coast." We went on to "from pole to pole," and soon will be speaking of "from planet to planet." All within a lifetime!

Does all this suggest that at long last we have come into a setting where the magnificent tradition of the prophets has little chance of being heard amidst the cacophony of authorities in a diverse secular time?

What we are saying here is that the very ground upon which the prophets historically have stood is the ground the secular world leaves out! For the secular, by definition, is life organized apart from God. The biblical prophets rested their case on the sovereignty of God over *all* of life. The secular world assumes that if God has sovereignty, it is over the realm called religious. The rest of life has its own sovereignties. The religious is God's domain.

This was revealed vividly to me in an experience in years past when I was pastor in a university center. It was still the custom to have a Religious Emphasis Week. We brought speakers who addressed the university from the standpoint of religion. To this, some of the "best minds" on the campus responded, "Well, these people have authority in the realm of religion, but they have little to say to the other fields of human endeavor, especially the scientific." So one year we took a different tack. We invited Professor Arthur Compton of the University of Chicago, an eminent physicist and a thoroughly committed Christian, to our campus for the week. He spoke brilliantly and simply about the meaning of faith. But again the "best minds" responded, "Well, of course, he's an authority in the field of physics, but he has no special qualification in the field of religion!" In our time, believe me, the tower of Babel is no myth. Where then shall the prophet stand, and what language shall he or she speak?

The Contemporary Prophet

This is a question of urgency. It would be an incomparable tragedy if the rich tradition of the prophets came to an end in our culture. It would be a tragedy because this is a culture where we so desperately *need* to know where the moral foundations of life really are. With our kind of problems, problems that literally can be called of life or death, we hunger for the sound of the prophet throughout the land. But can it be? Concerning this, two observations can be made.

First, it must be said that as the early prophet addressed the nation of Israel, the contemporary prophet must address the church. There *is* a covenant community. There *is* a "new nation" for whom the authoritative word is, "Thus saith the Lord." There *is* a people who are constantly struggling to understand the meaning of their covenant and who repeatedly must be brought back to it. So the first word of the prophet must be addressed to the church.

Can we then expect the church, in turn, to take a prophetic role in society? At first glance that seems like a rather meager hope. The church has resisted change far more often than it has supported it, it seems. But we had better look again. The church also has an amazing way not only of *sustaining* the values of life, but also, on occasion, of speaking with an impressive voice to change them. To be sure, the society tends to say to the church, "Keep quiet, put your hand upon your mouth, and come with us." But there are times when the prophetic ministry has emerged, as in Germany, for example, when a significant remnant of the church was the sole voice pointing out the evils of Nazism. In this country it seems fair

to say that it was the voice of the churches which helped
decide the issue of the civil rights bill. Even on those occasions
when the church as such has fallen short of its prophetic role,
it still has been the soil which produced the prophets.

*Secondly, we must recognize that the prophets in the
secular day may not use the language of faith, but they still
address the values which faith long ago established in our
common life.* This would be true of prophetic figures like
E. F. Schumacher in economics, Martin Luther King, Jr., in
racial justice, Mark Hatfield in politics, Dag Hammarskjöld in
international relations. It will not be surprising if the church
often finds itself in partnership with those who never use the
language of the biblical faith but have tried to keep the *ethic.*
Secularism which has been leavened by the biblical faith is
very different from the secularism which knows only materialism and the politics of power. So it is not only politics but
also prophecy which makes strange bedfellows!

Four Contemporary Concerns

What then is the prophetic message in a secular order?
The prophets will speak, it seems to me, of at least *four*
things.

First, they will speak of our *idolatry.* The secularism we
experience is not fundamentally atheistic, but polytheistic.
The reformers were given to saying that whatever our hearts
cling to or rely upon, that properly is our God. And our hearts
cling to many things. Our goods often become our gods.

In no place is this seen more vividly than in our advertising. Material things are pressed upon us not for what they do,
but for what they do *for us;* there is a promised spiritual result
from material possession. Like the man who went out to look
at his full barn and said, "Now, my soul, take thine ease," we
look at our material things and hope to be delivered. Jesus
said of the man in the parable, "Thou fool."

And what of us? In our secular world a car is advertised
as "something to believe in"; a soft drink is "the real thing."
Then there's the amazing promise, "Datsun saves. It sets you
free." In our time we have learned an old truth, namely, that
the alternative to belief in the God of the biblical faith is not
a high-minded humanism. It is the resurgence of old idolatries, a whole shelfful of household gods: success, sex, self,

materialism, before whom we bow down and say, "Thou art my god. Save me." We have many other gods before God.

Second, the prophets will speak of *judgment*. It may not be the judgment of an Old Testament God who rains down fire from heaven, though that is a sobering possibility for us. That kind of judgment is illustrated by the words of Julia Ward Howe's hymn:

Mine eyes have seen the glory of the coming of the Lord;
He has trampled out the vintage where the grapes of wrath are stored;
He has loosed the fateful lightning of His terrible swift sword. . . .

That's judgment. We'd know that a mile off.

But there is another kind, pervasive, inexorable, running all through the contemporary culture. It is summarized in the Bible's words about Samson when the Philistines were upon him: "He woke up, thinking, 'I shall get off as I have done over and over again . . .' not knowing that the Eternal had left him" (Judges 16:20, Moffatt).

"Not knowing that the Eternal had left him." Professor Tillich once raised an interesting question, "Could it be that, in order to judge the misuse of His name within the church, God reveals Himself from time to time by creating silence about Himself?"[4] So one day we found ourselves talking about the death of God. Incredible! We shall not be judged for talking about the death of God. That *is* the judgment—the sense of absence. When we are aware of God's absence, at least we are aware of God. It is judgment bringing us back. That judgment is upon us.

Third, the prophets shall speak also of *grace*. When did we surrender to the idea that the prophetic word is always laying people out for their sins? It equally is lifting people up from them! The prophetic word was overwhelmingly one of hope as well as judgment: "Ho, every one that thirsteth, come ye to the waters . . ." (Isaiah 55:1, KJV).

The word of grace is so needed because our secular day is under its own kind of law, at least as burdensome as the law under which Paul lived. For ours is the law of self-suffi-ciency. Our law is that we *ought* to be self-sufficient, and our gospel is that we *can* be. From that false law and false gospel emerges an unimaginable burden of human suffering. Joseph Wood Krutch once made a discerning comment about the drama he saw in New York. He said that contemporary

plays basically are rejecting the classic statement about grace
and saying instead, "'Since there is no God to grant the grace,
there in fact I am.'"⁵ To proclaim grace to a graceless society
caught in the downward spiral of the law of self-sufficiency is
a prophetic word—and a saving one.

Fourth, the prophets will speak of *resurrection.* How
strange that we've forgotten that the prophetic word is one
of ultimate and invincible hope! The first image we have of
the prophet is of one thundering judgment. But the fuller
picture is of the prophet proclaiming hope when there seems
no hope, and light in the midst of despair, because God's will
does prevail.

For those of us who preach today, the prophetic word is
not *less* assured than that of the Old Testament prophets; it
is *more.* For we preach on this side of the resurrection! To
the prophetic word of the Old Testament has been added the
consummate word of the New Testament. In the resurrection
came the showdown disclosure. Even out of death comes life.

The need for that daring word today is starkly apparent.
For other hopes have failed. Early in my ministry, science was
the hope. Scientists were saying essentially: "Just give us
time." By that they meant that in time they would fulfill the
best and highest hopes of humankind. Today speakers for
that same science are saying, "Just give us time." Now they
mean, "Give us time before the end." In the encircling gloom,
science has little hope. But the *prophetic* word *is* one of hope,
and it is desperately needed. It is the audacious affirmation
that in God's own way, in God's own time, God will prevail!
There are no other gods beside the Lord.

The Honor of God

"Keep quiet, put your hand upon your mouth, and come
with us." The world often promises great things to those who
will accept that compromise. But the inner compulsion that
took us into the ministry in the first place will not allow it.

Jean Anouilh's contemporary play *Becket* carries an interesting conversation between the King and Becket, who was
supposed to be his puppet Archbishop. Becket, having been
made Archbishop in order to serve as tool of the King, discovers that something is happening to him. He says to the
puzzled and angry King, "I am no longer like myself." To
which the King replies in sarcasm, "Have you been touched

by grace?" "Not by the one you think," says Becket. "What then?" demands the King. Then Becket replies, "I felt for the first time that I was being entrusted with something, that's all—there in that empty cathedral, somewhere in France, that day when you ordered me to take up this burden, I was a man without honor. And suddenly I found it—one I never imagined would ever become mine—the honor of God. A frail, incomprehensible honor, vulnerable as a boy-King fleeing from danger."[6]

Deep within each of us is the prayer that when the time demands, we may honor the name of the One who called us and speak the word that needs to be heard. To be sure, in the day-by-day ministry of the pastor such times of ultimate demand may come only on a few occasions in a lifetime. Even these occasions will not come unless one has been faithful in the lesser moral judgments which are a constant part of life.

But sometimes, some showdown times when the moral issues come down to either/or, one may have to settle the issue on "the honor of God." It is in *that* moment the preacher can speak the inescapable prophetic word, a moment when the calling actually is fulfilled with integrity and honor.

CHAPTER 3

The Preaching Encounter

Years ago, at the gentle prodding of my wife, I tried my hand at oil painting. Ever since, there have been flurries of artistic activity. The world at large, however, will have no problem getting along without my contributions! The most my artistic effort will contribute may be some good hours of personal pleasure. But those are a gift in themselves.

There have been other gifts, by-products of my occasional painting. One, of course, is an immensely heightened appreciation of the real masters—a kind of awe of their gifts and skills. Another is an enhanced ability to see shadows and lights and configurations. Included in those gifts is the understanding of the importance of perspective. One learns that every picture has a focal point, a center to which all other elements must be related. From the determination of that focal point, perspective takes form.

Any view we have of the Christian ministry must make a similar determination. Is there a focal point, and if so, what is it? Without that, the ministry falls into a kind of disorder. We may be able to name the various elements that go into the ministry, but we are not able to say how they relate to one another.

In our tradition, it seems to me we have an answer which has persisted for many generations, namely, that the focal point of the Christian ministry is preaching. It may be called proclamation or witnessing or exposition of the Word. Whatever we may name it, we cannot understand who we are without the recognition that by deliberate choice preaching is at the center of the Christian ministry, as we have understood it. There may be various ways of preaching the Word, but it is almost inconceivable that there could be ministry without some proclamation.

We have to carry that further, for preaching in our concept has a special meaning. It is not merely an act of human address. It is a time of *divine* address. It is not only the word of men *about* God, but it is also the word *of* God addressed to men. As Karl Barth has put it, the preachers are those who seek to answer the questions people may put to them, but also preachers are responding to the questions God puts to them. When that happens, asks Barth, what event is more momentous?[1] It is the conviction that, in spite of many evidences to the contrary, *preaching is something momentous—* a sacramental moment, as it were—which makes it the center of our corporate worship. We believe God has chosen preaching as a means of disclosure and grace.

One can say this quite easily as a theology of preaching. But when we move from that affirmation to the actual preaching we have experienced, we seem quickly to be brought back to earth. Much of the preaching we have known is dull and repetitious. Some of it shows slovenly and careless study habits of the preacher. Sometimes it seems to glorify the preacher far more than God. Some of it is incredibly removed from life as we know it day by day. When we see these things, we wonder if the claims for preaching are not simply proud illusions and if the hope of having a ministry in which preaching is central is not a futile one in our secular time. At the very least we need to reexamine the nature of the preaching encounter and to ask whether its claims are still valid in our secular day.

Divine Dimensions of Preaching

The belief that preaching has divine dimensions and is an event rather than a mere happening has very deep roots. Once while raking my yard I saw a twig which I tried to brush aside. When it would not yield to my rake, I tried to pick it up and toss it aside. But the harder I tried to throw it away, the more of it appeared. It proved to be not a twig at all but the exposed end of a tree root. That thing had connections! So even on those days when preaching seems a passing moment of no real significance, we need to remember—that thing has connections! Even the humblest occasion of gathering and speaking is the near end of a great affirmation centuries old. Preaching is, as P. T. Forsyth once put it, "the Gospel prolonging and declaring itself."[2]

That belief, of course, is deeply rooted in the New Testament. There the faith is explicit and clear. ". . . it pleased God through the folly of what we preach to save those who believe" (1 Corinthians 1:21). Few references appear more often than the reports that early believers went daily to the synagogue or the marketplace, teaching and preaching. Their message was the resurrection as the manifestation of God's sanction upon a particular man, Jesus of Nazareth. From the temple in Jerusalem to the Appian Way in Rome to Mars Hill in Athens, they laid the foundations of the church by preaching.

In one important way their preaching differed from ours. Often the preaching *followed* some manifestation of God's power. At Pentecost, Peter's sermon followed the evidences of the coming of the Spirit. At the temple, the sermon followed the healing of the impaired man. Our sermons, in contrast, often seem to say, *If only we would do this, then this would follow.* New Testament preaching said, "That which we have seen and heard declare we unto you . . ." (1 John 1:3, KJV). What you have seen, we now will interpret for you.

But it is important to note that even when the event had taken place, as at Pentecost or the healing at the temple, *these events did not speak for themselves.* They did not make preaching unnecessary; they made it even more imperative. The event was not complete until interpretation had taken place. Preaching was a part of the acts of the apostles.

While it is clear beyond dispute that the early church depended upon preaching for evangelism, the urgent task of winning new believers, the question still remains about the place preaching had in those times when the church gathered for praise and remembrance of Jesus Christ. Was preaching part of that primitive liturgy? In short, did they have preaching in church or only out of it? For some answers to that we are dependent, of course, on Paul's letters, for here we see, sometimes directly, sometimes by implication, what life in the New Testament churches must have been. Of course, we have one insight in the book of Acts where it is recorded that a certain Eutychus went to sleep while Paul was preaching! Some of us, thinking of similar times in our own congregation, can take wry comfort from that scene! It happened even to the apostle Paul! Apparently that preaching was going on in the gathered church. We know that the church observed the Agape meal and the Lord's Supper. We know that in the believers' times of gathering they often experienced charismatic gifts. We know that they took offerings for distressed brothers and sisters. But was preaching a regular practice?

Again we are dependent upon references and allusions in the letters which passed from church to church. Some scholars feel that the "prophecy" referred to in chapter 12 of First Corinthians may have been the nearest to what we call preaching. In the Pastoral Epistles the word in Second Timothy seems to reflect the seriousness with which they took interpretation and exposition, "Do your best to present yourself to God as one approved, a workman who has no need to be ashamed, rightly handling the word of truth" (2:15). One of Paul's expressed concerns was the "edification" of the church. When one considers the care with which Paul dealt with the theological foundations on which the new churches were founded, it seems inconceivable that they did not give regular interpretation when the believers gathered. Our preaching roots are indeed in the New Testament.

It was the Reformation which specifically put the preaching of the Word as the focal point of Christian worship. The central place which had been held by the mass in the Catholic service—the sacramental moment—passed to the preaching of the Word. Here was the time when the great expectancy came to its fullest height, the elevation not of the host, but of the Word. Here was the time when God was most clearly known to be present. So the reformers said, "Where the Word of God is preached and the sacraments administered, there is the church." In some sense, the pulpit replaced the altar. In Calvin's Geneva it was required to attend and hear the Word of God.

We have the record of one Monsieur Jean Balard, who refused to go to church. When he was asked if he didn't want to hear the Word of God, he replied that he would be glad to hear the Word of God but he certainly wasn't going to hear those preachers! He was placed in prison with a specific instruction that once a week he was to be taken under guard to the preaching service, where he was required to hear the Word preached.[3] Unfortunately, we have no record of the success of this compulsory evangelism! But we may speculate with some assurance that it was somewhat lacking in its efficacy.

These days are 450 years behind us, but they have left their mark on our day, too. Preaching, more than any part of the service, still is expected to be the momentous event, something out of the ordinary. We still feel the prompting of a tradition whose roots may have been lost but which gives us the feeling that when the Bible is opened and the preaching begins, the main business is going on.

This belief found its own form in Baptist practice. John Bunyan's imprisonment for eleven years was largely because he refused to promise that he would not preach. It was a significant scene when his congregation greeted him as he came out of prison. The first thing they did was to go to a nearby barn where they could hear a sermon! John Robinson, in 1620, assured his newborn Baptist congregation in Holland that "'the Lord [has] more truth and light yet to breake forth out of his holy Word.'"[4] There seems ample evidence that Baptists from the beginning sought the new light by the practice of preaching.

The Real Power in Preaching

Now we must move on to deal with another aspect of our inquiry. It seems important to ask why we expect so much of preaching. Does it imply that the preaching exercise itself is a source of power? Is it a kind of evocative ritual, the exercise of which calls out redemptive powers? What is preaching supposed to do that justifies its central place in our corporate life?

Two points should be made to clarify the Protestant or Free Church tradition. The first is that we do not cherish preaching for its own sake but because it is a means by which Christ is allowed to do his work among us. The power is not in preaching, as such, but in the Christ who is preached. There is no power inherent in preaching, as though the exercise itself had some mysterious efficacy. Preaching is central because it is a way by which a living Christ is released again into our personal and common life. Preaching is made the focal point because Christ is the focal point, and we believe that where the Word of Christ is preached, the work of Christ goes on.

As is so often true, it is the apostle Paul who gives us the image we need. In the classic Second Corinthians passage he says, "So we are ambassadors for Christ, God making his appeal through us . . ." (5:20). Ambassadors! The figure gathers up so much of what we have been saying. An ambassador represents another, having neither power nor identity apart from the one who gives the ambassador his or her credentials. Often his or her purpose is to effect a meeting between those to whom he or she is sent and the one who did the sending. An ambassador is, in simplest terms, a go-between, establishing a relationship. In that sense, the preacher *is* an ambassador for Christ. The preacher's purpose is to bring meeting between those to whom he or she is sent and the One in whom the power actually resides.

Or again, we will find a helpful image of the preaching encounter in the Gospel narrative of the walk to Emmaus. In many ways, effective preaching is a walk home on the Emmaus Road. It begins where the need is, as in the case of the disciples who set out from Jerusalem to go to Emmaus, heavy in heart and emptied of their great hope. " 'But we had hoped that he was the one . . .'" (Luke 24:21). It then tries to make it possible for Christ to fall into stride and walk with us, often unrecognized at first, but interpreting the meaning of our experience. Then we come back home, to a familiar and loved place where the new disclosure takes place. "Their eyes were opened and they recognized him . . ." (v. 31). Yet such disclosures are passing. ". . . he vanished out of their sight" (v. 31). The disclosure in a sermon may seem short-lived. But life is different because of it. ". . . 'Did not our hearts burn within us while he talked to us on the road . . .?'" (v. 32). No, they didn't, but already the downheartedness with which they began the journey had been redeemed, turned into victory. And the end of it? "They rose that same hour and returned to Jerusalem . . ." (v. 33). An effective sermon is, indeed, a walk on the road to Emmaus.

To say that the preaching encounter in its fullest is mediating the power of Christ to human life is not to narrow the message, but only to focus it. Preaching that mediates Christ moves in a rich and broad field. It must know the richness of the Old Testament, for there are the roots of Christ, the re-markable faith that produced him. It must speak often of the church as the believing and loving community which was the fruit of his life and death and resurrection. Then, of course, that preaching will go again and again to his ministry upon earth, all with a purpose of showing the amplification of life which waits for us now in him. That does not narrow our preaching. It only gives us eyes to see the whole event of Jesus Christ, measured not in a few years, but in the centuries.

But, again, the persistent question: Can we really expect preaching to do that? Isn't it too didactic and lifeless? Much of it is. But does anything offer a better potential? Is there anything that combines as many elements for imparting life? Take the wonder of words, for example. They are among our most priceless possessions. By a word, human experience is imparted. A word can speak of love or call out hate; it can comfort or arouse fear; it can call forth laughter or tears; it can bring people together or set them apart; it can heal or hurt. The power of words is incalculable.

At the same time consider the impact of person upon person. Nothing compares with it. We love only because someone first loved us. We fall in love not in principle but in person. Most of the causes which we serve enlisted us because we met someone whom that cause had claimed. The best things in life are person to person.

So preaching uses both these elements: the wonder of words and the impact of persons. Both are part of Phillips Brooks's classic definition that preaching is "truth through personality."[5] What is more manifestly sacramental than a warm human relationship which consistently is under obe-dience to God? Of course, preaching carries no guarantee, and much of it falls far short of that which it might be. But it can be an instrument of immense promise, and the belief that God has chosen to use that instrument for his purposes seems to me well grounded in human experience.

Sometimes what surprises of grace there are! On a snowy day in London a young man, finding he could not get to his Baptist church, stopped at a nearby Methodist church. Be-cause the minister couldn't get there, a layman got up and preached the sermon. But that was the moment when God's grace overflowed for that young man, and he was converted. His name was Charles Haddon Spurgeon. Who can name the moment? Who can say when any sermon fits into God's agenda? Some soul may go to church one day thinking that that action is, like Jesus' going to the synagogue in Nazareth (Luke 4:16), only according to his or her custom. That may be the very day when the momentous event takes place. God addresses us, and the sermon proves to be the earthen vessel which carries the treasure. There has always been a mystery about the preaching encounter. We can describe it, but we cannot fully explain it. All life must acknowledge the essential mysteries by which we live. In the practice of our faith, preaching is still the mystery of our corporate worship.

The Discipline of Preaching

Yet preaching is a demanding mystery. We are not released from considerations of our workmanship. To the contrary: in every realm of life, the greater the power the more is required of those who use it. After these years of trying to be obedient to the preaching ministry, there are three summary observations I have chosen to make.

First, to speak of God's activity in the preaching encounter is not to imply our inactivity. Perhaps the greatest shortcoming of our preaching is the failure to accept the disciplines that go with the claim. To preach a sermon that shows obvious signs of undisciplined thinking or which reveals that the preacher has not come to terms with his or her own ego needs is to deny, by the performance, what is claimed by the profession. It reflects not only ''cheap grace'' but also an essential cynicism. It assumes that the power of God can be used to our own ends. We all fall short of being what we ought to be, but that does not release us from trying. I'm concerned about preaching which never gets to the point of grace, for it doesn't even go as far as works can go. To say that the preaching encounter is momentous because of the possibility that God will use it for divine purposes is not a release from study, preparation, and devotions, but a reason for them. It is the hope that gives the discipline meaning.

One thinks of this sometimes when one sees a violinist take time to tune his or her instrument once more before beginning to play. The greater the music and the musician, the more important a tuned instrument becomes. The artist cannot say, "This is Beethoven's work and there is none greater. It will come through because it is Beethoven." The sheer profundity of the music makes it even more imperative that the instrument be finely tuned.

Even more so a preacher cannot say, "But this is the Word of God. Who can frustrate God?" We can! An undisciplined preacher is an untuned instrument. The final confirmation of our claim is to see what God can do with the preacher who has sought to be a finely tuned instrument of God's grace.

Second, since we are dealing here with the practice of preaching, a further observation seems in order. It is the hope that the insight contained in the phrase "life situation preaching" will not be lost by those of us who believe that preaching is basically biblical.

There is no reason to assume, as some do, that these are alternative ways of preaching, set off against each other. The real question is not whether preaching addresses the life situation, but what it brings to that situation. We may assume, I think, that since God addressed the human situation in the incarnation, we can do no less! God's word, while biblical and transcendent, must come to us where we are, in our common human experiences; that means in crises, in the facing of death and grief, in decisions, in the experiences of alienation and forgiveness, and in our need to find daily strength. Though we believe preaching goes far beyond human experience, it is never less than that.

The weakness (or better, corruption) of life situation preaching has been that it so easily becomes an exercise in problem solving. God is not to be cherished as the solver of problems but as the sovereign Lord of life, problems and all. It is the magnificent truth of the Bible that God's great disclosures are in our common life. Preaching must deal with life as it is, for there we find God as God is. It can be in the darkest of experiences, the depth of despair or guilt or grief, or it can be in the wonder of some unexpected victory or in the celebration of life. Here is where the gospel confronts us. The preaching encounter begins in acknowledging the real and present life situations.

We sometimes do not recognize that the Gospel of Luke speaks of two transfigurations, not one. The first, of course, was on the mountaintop when the experience was extraordinary, a vision given to very few. But the second transfiguration came when they went down into the valley and immediately were faced with a poignant human situation, the

anguish of a distraught father over his stricken son. There
the record has a magnificent truth, simply stated. It says that
when the child was healed, "All were astonished at the majesty
of God" (Luke 9:43). That's where the majesty of God is seen
by most of us. Given the choice between a mountaintop experience which few could have, on the one hand, and the
healing of a child, on the other, we would choose the child
every time, no contest. Preaching should speak of that second
transfiguration given us in life situations.

My third observation relates to the effectiveness of
preaching. It is often felt that sermons have no visible results.
Many of us cannot point to any one sermon that "changed
my life." To be sure, some sermons do change life suddenly.
But for most of us preaching is a part of an ongoing life, and
it seems only habitual and pedestrian.

Yet, for this moment, I would speak for the place preaching has in our lives on a *sustaining* basis. Like most nourish-
ment it is strength for the day and renewal for our common
tasks. Perhaps preaching must be judged by Isaiah's words:

> "For as the rain and the snow come down from heaven,
> and return not thither but water the earth,
> making it bring forth and sprout,
> giving seed to the sower and bread to the eater,
> so shall my word be that goes forth from my mouth;
> it shall not return to me empty. . . ."
>
> —Isaiah 55:10-11

The Personal Encounter

Perhaps it is time to return to the key word of this
chapter—encounter. Ever since Emil Brunner first spoke of
the "divine-human encounter,"[6] the phrase has seemed to
me aptly descriptive of preaching itself.

Actually, "encounter" has two seemingly contradictory
meanings. The first is "to meet in opposition, to engage in
conflict." When one considers the nature of our human experiences, there is a large place for such preaching, because
evil and sin, indeed, must be met and engaged at times.
Perhaps this is one aspect of the prophetic role.

The other meaning of "encounter," however, is "to come
upon face to face" and certainly that has a precise meaning
when we are speaking of preaching. It must be intimate,
personal, and face to face. This may be the pastoral aspect

of our task. Because of both meanings we fittingly speak of the preaching encounter.

Both aspects of it seem vividly described in Monica's words about Ambrose, as related in Samuel Valentine Cole's poem, "Monica: The Chronicle of Marcus." One only hopes that on occasion these words may fit the contemporary pulpit also.

> "I visit the cathedral now and then
> To hear the bishop, rhetoricians should;
> He has the art of it; I tell thee what,
> The people spread their ears out when he talks.
> And yet he is no trickster, as I think,
> No lank, wild-eyed and overholy saint,
> No splitter of hairs and juggler with the truth,
> No oily-mouthed emitter of fine speech,
> No loud volcano of cinders, smoke and mud—
> Varieties which I have sometimes found
> At Rome and elsewhere—he is none of these,
> But just a plain, whole-hearted, wholesome man,
> Of ample girth of body and mind, who speaks
> The truth straight out,—what he indeed calls truth
> And holds truth in the bottom of his soul.
> He speaks, then lets it work; and it does work;
> The man has powerful influence hereabouts;
> 'Tis said the devil himself throws up the job
> He may be working at when Ambrose comes."[7]

CHAPTER 4

The Mediating Community

One of the classics of our distinctively American literature is the novel *Moby Dick,* by Herman Melville. Set in the days when the whaling industry was an important part of the New England economy, it tells the story of a vessel in search of the White Whale. Many have felt it was the intention of Melville in writing this story to portray the struggle against evil.

One of the characters of the story is Father Mapple, the pastor of a church especially for those engaged in the whaling industry. There is a long description of a sermon which Father Mapple gave in that chapel. The pulpit was shaped like the prow of a ship with the Bible resting on the most forward part, what Melville called the "ship's fiddle-headed beak." Of this Melville says, "What could be more full of meaning?—for the pulpit is ever this earth's foremost part; all the rest comes in its rear; the pulpit leads the world. . . . Yes, the world's a ship on its passage out, and not a voyage complete; and the pulpit is its prow." [1]

Of special interest is the way in which Father Mapple entered the high pulpit of those times. Rather than ascending steps, he climbed into it by a ship's ladder, the kind they hang over the side so that people can board. Father Mapple slowly made his way up that ladder; then, once in the pulpit, he reached over and pulled the ladder up after him. Of this the author says, "Can it be, then, that by this act of physical isolation, he signifies his spiritual withdrawal for the time, from all outward worldly ties and connections?" This seems to Melville a most appropriate act, for he concludes, ". . . to the faithful man of God, this pulpit, I see, is a self-containing stronghold. . . ."[2]

For most of us, the first inclination is to approve and affirm this image. There is, indeed, a sense in which the pulpit must show its detachment from the things of the earth. It certainly cannot preach only what people want to hear, nor can it grant to anyone censorship of the Word of God. Like Father Mapple, when we enter the pulpit, we assume a certain detachment.

The image of the preacher has often gone back and forth between the prophetic and the heroic. Sometimes the faithful preacher has seemed heroic, standing up when others do not stand. Often the preacher has seemed prophetic, speaking from a position nearer God than anyone else, thundering on occasion, and gently persuading on others. Sometimes the preacher has been looked upon, as the people of Israel looked upon their high priest, as one who entered alone into the Holy of Holies and brought back word from the Almighty. Of course, there is a large measure of truth in all these images. In one sense, the preacher, like Father Mapple, does have to pull the ladder up.

Yet in my preaching pilgrimage the other side of this truth has addressed me with increasing meaning. The truth emerges that the preacher cannot be the preacher apart from the community of faith. At last one is brought to disagree with Melville's statement, "This pulpit is a self-containing stronghold." It is not self-containing or self-contained at all, nor is it a stronghold apart from the people of faith. It is even true to say that, in a deep sense, the *community* is the preacher, the proclaimer, the witness. To be sure, the one preaching is the speaker, but the Word is not anyone's personal possession. It is a word entrusted to a community of faith. It rarely is to be found when one enters the pulpit and pulls up the ladder. We cannot break family ties like that—and there *is* a family of faith!

This is a word which may bring forth reservations in free church circles. We may sense in this a threat to that most cherished of all our beliefs, "freedom of soul." Are we going to give any community jurisdiction over an individual's beliefs? Are we going to let any body of people determine what the preacher is to preach? These are real questions. But to ask these alone is to miss the point. What we are affirming is that there is no freedom in isolation, nor is truth to be found there. The preacher cannot be a kind of Simeon Stylites, high on the pillar of his pulpit, sending down messages from God. The whole New Testament simply pulsates with the concept of the community of faith, the new nation, the new family, the new covenant, the body of believers.

In the hope that it will be helpful, we need to explore more deeply the relation between the preacher and that community of faith. For there is both a new freedom and a new strength to be found in that freshened understanding. We shall deal, first of all, with the nature of the community and, second, with the nature of the preacher's relationship to it.

Four Contributions of the Community

Giving our consideration to the first point, there are four essentials for preaching which only a believing community can provide. Without these, preaching could not take place at all.

First, there is the obvious truth that it takes a community to *transmit* the gospel. Without it, the preacher would not have received the very word he or she preaches. "What have you that you did not receive?" (1 Corinthians 4:7) Paul asked the early church; the answer is as implied for us as it was for them.

Canon Alan Richardson points to the believing community as the first fact of the Christian faith. He says: "The *datum* of theology is as truly 'given' as the *datum* of physics: there *is* a believing and witnessing Church. . . . The task of theology, then, arises because of the existence of the worshipping and witnessing Christian community. . . ."[3] Free church experience often stresses the sense of immediacy. We need to add to it the experience of continuity. It is the community of believers that makes that continuity possible.

This seems such an obvious truth; yet it needs to be clarified. To say that the church is the means of transmitting the word may give the impression that it simply "passes it on." Our electronic age has many new examples of transmission. We dictate a statement into a machine, and the word is always there waiting for someone to come along and hear it exactly as it was received. To transmit it precisely as it first was given is the mark of "high fidelity."

But the transmission of the gospel is something really quite different. For each generation not only receives the gospel, but it also lives with it. What is transmitted is dynamic, not static. It requires each generation to say yes in its own terms and to make its own commitment. Those receiving must find *new* dimensions of meaning and on occasion decide what has become outmoded or anachronistic. The believing community not only receives what has been transmitted, but also it struggles with it and, out of that struggle, enhances it. It is that struggle which is passed on to the next generation. It assumes, as John Robinson put it, "the Lord [has] more truth and light yet to breake forth out of his holy Word!"⁴ But that new light cannot be found if the Word has not been transmitted. It is the community of the church, which, as Paul put it, has been "entrusted with the gospel" (1 Thessalonians 2:4). The majestic mystery of the gospel is that it is more than any generation understands; yet each generation can add its own dimension. It is important to emphasize, then, the dynamic nature of the Word which the community transmits. It is an energy, an audacity, a saving mystery which is transmitted, and it does its work in each generation. "The word of God is living and active . . . discerning the thoughts and intentions of the heart" (Hebrews 4:12).

History has many illustrations of this. In 1817 a meeting of Baptists was called in central New York for the purpose of establishing an educational society. There was a disappointing response. Only thirteen people showed up for the meeting! Rather than abandon the attempt, however, they moved from the church to the nearby home of a deacon and went on with the meeting. They had come with a purpose and they intended to see it through. They wanted to form an educational society that would help provide a learned ministry for the young churches established in that area.

It is interesting to note that of the thirteen present only one had a college education. All the rest, however, believed in it and wanted to provide for others what they did not have themselves. Tradition says that they gave thirteen prayers and thirteen dollars, and the society was established. Now we look back upon that distant day and see an amazing phenomenon.

From that society, founded by thirteen people who felt it important to transmit the good news of the church, there came forth two universities, Colgate University and the University of Rochester and a theological school, Colgate Rochester Divinity School. From these institutions have gone forth thousands of men and women who benefited from a concern transmitted that day by thirteen people.

The church has known many times when the most it could do was to conserve the Word and keep it alive for a better day, like a farmer conserving his seed in the winter. Again and again it has taken the responsibility for seeing that the trust is kept through some wintertime of history, confidently believing seedtime will come again. Under the realities in which many Christians today live, it often seems not possible to transmit the gospel abroad as we would like. Yet it still is a ministry to be faithful and to keep that Word intact for the day when it can move out more fully into our common life.

Again, it takes a community to express the *diversity* of the faith. How eloquently Paul put it! "Now there are varieties of gifts, but the same Spirit; and there are varieties of service, but the same Lord; and there are varieties of working, but it is the same God who inspires them all in every one" (1 Corinthians 12:4-5). Then, having noted the diversity, he expresses his faith about the meaning of it. "To each is given the manifestation of the Spirit for the common good" (1 Corinthians 12:7). In short, diversity is not for competition but for completion. Without our brothers and sisters none of us can be made whole, nor can the mission of the church be carried through. Only a *community* of believers has the gifts that make the mission possible.

Sometimes one sees a parable of this at a concert. Before the program begins, the players in the orchestra come casually to their places and begin to warm up their instruments. What an amazing diversity there is, a veritable cacophony of sound! But as the moment for beginning comes, a silence descends. A conductor steps forth from the wings, holds up the baton, and out of cacophony comes symphony! The diversity is now for enrichment. The whole orchestra is needed to produce the music.

Carry this figure of speech for a moment over into the church. It may help illustrate how it takes the full community to receive and live through the Word which preaching proclaims. It takes many gifts, not one. It takes diversity, not uniformity. Each of us has an individual response to the Word preached, of course, but it requires the whole community for full response, for God uses our diversity.

We have learned, for example, that mission requires diverse gifts. That has become manifestly true in our day. The mission at home and abroad calls upon all kinds of gifts, from the practical to the spiritual, from the theological to the technical, from the humane to the scientific. The mission to the world may be carried for a while by some heroic man or woman of faith; but in due time it has to become the work of the whole community. The needs are diverse, more so than we ever knew, and so must the gifts to meet those be diverse, too.

Also, our knowledge of God requires diverse testimony. God is so beyond all that we ask or think that we welcome every testimony. We hear many words, that in them we might find the Word. To me, that is the ongoing excitement of the church of Jesus Christ. It hears our testimony and adds it to the mounting witness of the whole church.

Christian worship is like a shared meal. Each of us brings some contribution and passes it around! We even may call this one kind of Lord's Supper! One comes saying, "I have some faith this week and I would like to share it with you." Another brings courage, or joy, or freshened experience of God. Then we pass it around to all, a shared meal of faith. What we know about God is the witness we bear to one another in the community of faith! It, too, is one of the gifts of diversity!

Once more, the church is needed for *nurturing* the Word of Christ. For the Word received has to go on growing. The preacher without the church is like a farmer without a field. He only can scatter the seed abroad, knowing that much of it will fall on stony ground indeed. We believe that if God ordained the preacher to proclaim the Word, God also ordained the community to receive it and nurture it. Most preachers can tell in short order whether the listening congregation has a sense of its ordination. Perhaps one of the greatest ministries we can have to our congregations is to help them discover that sense of their ordination. For that nurturing church is the context in which real preaching comes.

We always experience sadness when we see that our nurturing has failed. In 1835 a young man wrote an essay for his university application in Germany. It was a theme entitled "A Young Man's Choice of His Career." In it he warned that a young man was not to leave his career to chance but should listen to the inner voice, the guidance of God. The essay was in a pious vein through and through. It declared that all men have a deep need for religious comfort. It affirmed, moreover, that everyone has a nature inclined to sin, a fallible mind, a spoiled heart, and is an outcast from the face of God, but he can exult in his Redeemer. It is recorded that the examiners were very much impressed by this essay, written by a seventeen-year-old. They received him into the university, happy for the moral tone of such writing.

But it needs to be recorded that the young man's name was Karl Marx, and time proved that the seed had fallen on very shallow soil indeed. One cannot help wondering what would have happened if the church had seen through its nurturing mission more effectively.

There is a fourth consideration which seems to me important for the relation between the community and preaching; namely, some aspects of the Word preached assume a *covenant* community. As you cannot understand the Old Testament prophet apart from the covenant Israel had with God, neither can you understand the Christian preacher apart from the covenant shared by members of the community of Christ. As the prophet constantly appealed to the covenant, often calling Israel back to it, the contemporary preacher will speak to the covenant we have with one another and with God in Christ.

This covenant relationship determines the nature of preaching. One sees this in the life of Paul. Paul, standing before Agrippa or on Mars Hill, preaches one way. But, standing in the midst of the believing community—those "in Christ"—he preaches another. To the latter he makes appeal; he sometimes admonishes; he often reminds his listeners; always he is the teacher. For he is speaking to those "in Christ." These are the people of the covenant. He speaks to them in terms of that covenant. He is addressing himself to the common loyalty, the commitment to which all have given themselves.

One must confess that this often seems to be a narrowing circle in our culture. To try to bring the gospel to the secular mind is to search and search for some point of contact. To speak of the faith by which we live to those who not only do not have that faith but also often feel no need for it is to sing the Lord's song in a strange land. Or to try to address the Christian gospel to those who already are under another commitment often leaves one with immense frustrations. As Reinhold Niebuhr once noted, there are those who "regard Christ 'as foolishness' because they have no questions for which Christ is the answer. . . ."[5] Today we can add he also is foolishness to those who think they have found the answer and discovered that it has nothing to do with Jesus Christ. To proclaim a saving Word to a secular mind which feels no need for it is our challenge. It brings us back with a tremendous sense of freedom to those to whom we can speak within a common covenant. The church provides that base, and we ought to be grateful for it.

In this concept of the covenant is the answer, it seems to me, to those preachers who fear that the emphasis upon the importance of the community will threaten their individual freedom. By its very nature, the covenant is *voluntary* through and through. It is not a concentration of power but a confession of common obedience.

In any free church there are two essential freedoms. One, of course, is the freedom of the pulpit. A congregation cannot tell preachers what they must preach or what they may not. It may want to, on occasion, but the respect for that freedom of the pulpit is an essential of our congregational life! But there is also freedom of the pew. The preacher cannot tell members of the congregation what they must believe or what they may not. The preacher cannot tell others they must attend or may not. Between these two freedoms, both expressions of the freedom of soul, we believe there is room for God to work, bringing forth that new light that is God's Word. To say that we are a covenanting community is a guarantee that both of those freedoms will be preserved.

The Relation of the Preacher to the Community

We must turn now to the central thesis with which we began, namely, that both the identity and effectiveness of the preacher are to be found in his or her relation to the community of faith. We have seen this as a transmitting, diverse, nurturing, and covenant community. Then what is the relation of the preacher to it?

Stated most simply, the preachers are related to the community of faith as trees are related to the soil: they have their roots in it and they plant their seed in it. The community is both the source and the conserver of preaching.

It can be said truthfully, then, that the *community* is really the preacher and the person in the pulpit is the spokesperson. To be sure, by the very freedom of which we have spoken, a preacher must put his or her own initials on the gospel he or she preaches. It is not enough to advocate, we must bear witness too. But the faith to which the preacher witnesses is the faith of the whole community, and in that sense it is the community itself which preaches.

There have emerged from time to time attempts to separate the preaching from the community itself. During the Reformation a burgher of Strasbourg, Peter Schott, left a sum of money to endow a preacher. He specified that he was to be a doctor of theology who had not taken the monk's vows but who on his own would preach to the people in the vernacular. A special pulpit was even erected in Strasbourg for the preacher provided by this foundation. An eloquent and scholarly man named John Geiler was chosen. But it is significant that the practice had its day and ceased to be. They learned again that, apart from the community, preaching denies its very nature.

One looks back over a lifetime of preaching and discovers that the community of faith means different things at different times. There has never been a time when I have been apart from the community of believers. But at different stages of life I see its meaning in different ways. When my ministry began, I especially appreciated the *stimulus* of the community and found it prophetic and even revolutionary. That is still an exciting part of it, but something else has been added. It now proves to be a source of *comfort.*

Karl Barth once said, in the late years of his life, " 'I often have to fight with a quite inexplicable sadness in which all the success that life has brought me is *no use at all.* ' " [6] From the time Moses had to climb Mount Nebo and look over into the Promised Land into which he would never enter, that has been a feeling that confronts anyone near the close of ministry. It is simply unfinished business all the way!

But because of the community of believers one hopes that some seed has been planted which yet may bear fruit.

We may hope that God has provided the community in order that the unfinished business may go on.

That's a moving word which closes chapter 11 of Hebrews. After calling the roll of the great heroes of faith the writer said, "All these died not having received the promise." At first you protest—that is not fair. If they don't receive the promise, what chance have we? But we read on, "Since God had foreseen something better . . . that apart from us they should not be made perfect."

It is that ongoing community which we celebrate. It is that community in which we find our homeland as preachers of the gospel.

CHAPTER 5

The Pain of Preaching

There seems to be an unwritten agreement that when preachers speak of their calling, they should always think in terms of its privilege. We prefer to think of the pulpit as one place "where seldom is heard a discouraging word and the skies are not cloudy all day"!

That it *is* a privilege, most of us vigorously would affirm. In its highest moments preaching leaves one standing in awe before its dignity, even its majesty. But this does not mean that there is no pain in it. Moreover, that pain is not something which really can be eliminated. It is not a sign that something has gone wrong, but rather a sign that all is going about as expected. Anyone who has not known times of pain in the preaching ministry probably has yet to come to terms with the tension between the calling as it is meant to be and the world as it really is. Some of us could testify that out of those very times of pain have come some of the most cherished insights and strengths of the Christian ministry.

Paul often confessed to finding pain in his calling. He fell so far short of what he wanted to be: ". . . for what I would, that do I not; but what I hate, that do I" (Romans 7:15, KJV). He knew the burden of sin in his own life: "O wretched man that I am! who shall deliver me . . .?" (Romans 7:24, KJV).

One of the finest insights, however, is found in the second letter to the Corinthians. Paul felt that he had caused the Corinthian church a great deal of pain. For one thing, he had to chastise them by letter, and he was sure that had caused them grief. Moreover, he had promised to come see them but had failed to do so. He was sure this also caused them no little pain. He may have been a little naive about that!

Even so, out of this minor setting there came a tremendous insight into the significance of pain. Paul then wrote, ". . . the pain God is allowed to guide ends in a saving repentance never to be regretted . . ." (2 Corinthians 7:10, Moffatt).

Every word is significant. "The pain *God is allowed to guide.*" That is no bland promise that everything will come out all right. There is a condition, "the *pain God is allowed to guide* ends in a saving repentance." That doesn't say it comes automatically or even immediately. *"Ends* in a saving repentance." "Never to be regretted." That is a view in retrospect, an outcome greatly to be desired.

Is it then really possible that the pain which is in the ministry thus can be redeemed? Can it become, as promised, a source of power and insight?

To answer that, we will need to be more specific about the pains of preaching. There are some, of course, which are temporary, symptoms of the times when we are alienated from our work. But there are some pains which are always with us, because they are intrinsic. They go with the territory, as it were! It is those pains to which we need to give deeper attention.

The Pain of Incompletion

The first is *the pain of incompletion.* Of course, that is true of life itself. Everyone experiences what Phillips Brooks called "the withheld completions of life."[1] But for the preacher it is a way of life. All our years we must deal with the immeasurable and the imprecise. In an age which practices evaluation, measures results, and expects annual reports, this "rounding out" is denied the preacher. How can you measure what we're really about? Oh, we have our reports, of course! But they cannot measure the primary things, the distinctive realities. Can you say, "We are happy to report that we were 19 percent more loving this year than last"? Can you add that 23 percent more people received comfort this year, or, conversely, sadly confess that our experience of God declined 10 percent? We have to become reconciled to imprecision and incompletion because that's the nature of the reality with which we deal. In a secular culture that often is a painful condition to accept.

If our ears have not been closed by the familiarity of the words, we ought to be amazed at the way in which chapter 11 of Hebrews comes to a close. It relates the acts of faith of an amazing group of heroes. What a story of the courage and devotion of men and women who lived by faith is unfolded! But at the close it says, "And all these, though well attested by their faith, did not receive what was promised" (v. 39). You could say, and rightly, "That's not fair." Then you wonder what chance there is for us. If *they* didn't receive the promise, who will? But the next phrase affirms our faith, "Since God had foreseen something better for us." Better than completion? Yes, but it takes a deeper faith than we have known to accept failure in that faith.

Up in Canada, between the Thousand Islands and Montreal, is an area on the St. Lawrence River called Lachine Rapids. "Lachine," of course, in French means China. What in the world is China doing in the middle of Canada? It goes back to that distant day when the first explorers sailed up the St. Lawrence and came to the place where the river narrowed into rapids. The explorers thought they had found what they were looking for: China! So they named it Lachine. Imagine! They only missed it by about nine thousand miles! How those who stayed cozily at home would have laughed at such a mistake! But the adventurous were basically right. There *is* a China, and it *can* be reached by water, and it *did* lie in that direction. What they did not know was that there were new worlds between them and their final destination. There was more to this world than they knew!

It takes a great faith to believe God has "foreseen something better." To stand before our incompletion and apparent failure, our mistakes and our inadequacies, and still to believe that God can use even these, is a faith for which we ought to pray daily.

One thinks of this in relation to Moses. What an injustice it was, it seems to us, that the man who led the people of Israel through the wilderness toward the Promised Land was not allowed to enter it himself. That's high tragedy and a moving moment when Moses stands on Mount Nebo and sees the Promised Land which he never will enter. Then was it all loss? Not at all. Moses never got into the Promised Land. But the Promised Land got into Moses! Do you doubt what that vision did for him? It took a stammering shepherd off the mountain, gave him the courage to confront a king. It took him from the care of sheep to the care of a people. It took him to Mount Sinai where he alone was granted the vision of what life lived with God ought to be. It enabled him to give a whole nation courage and stamina. He never was allowed to put his foot in the Promised Land. But his heart was in it all the time. That vision made the man, and the man made the nation.

It is in our preaching that we are most aware of "the withheld completions." Here we often will fall back upon Isaiah's vision of the word of God. For Isaiah proclaims God as promising, "My word shall not return to me empty" (see 55:11). Then he says that as the rain and the snow fall and water the earth and cause it to bring forth good things, seed for the sower and bread for the eater, so shall God's word be. The question is not whether the word brings results, but what results we have a right to expect. If the word itself disappears, it is like the snow and the rain falling into the earth. It already has disappeared to do its work. And in due time, by God's grace, it will bring forth seed for the sower and bread for the eater. But in the winter of our discouragement we often will know the pain of incompletion.

The Pain of Irrelevance

Second, we will need to speak of *the pain of irrelevance.* Now that does not mean we are irrelevant in our own eyes! But it does mean that a secular culture, by its very nature, tends to push us into the coffin corner. The easiest way for a secular culture to handle preachers is to confine them to a vague area called "the religious." Secularism, by definition, almost has eliminated the premise upon which the biblical faith rests, namely, the sovereignty of God over all of life. Secular culture insists upon business as business, art for art's sake, and often, my nation right or wrong. In the division of labor it has given the preacher a vague area which is partly otherworldly, partly nostalgia, and partly civil religion. In such a setting we often must feel the pain of noncontact. Secularism is a strange setting for the biblical faith—make no mistake about that.

This comes to its most poignant point for some of us in the preacher's attempt to address the youth in this generation. Alan Valentine has compiled a book entitled *Fathers to Sons: Advice Without Consent*. In it he has brought together letters of fathers to sons in many generations, showing how difficult it always has been for one to understand the other. In his introduction, Valentine summarizes the findings thus:

> To every generation the succeeding one seems to be ignoring essential truths and values; to every new age its predecessor seems stodgy or hypocritical. . . . A father can barely stomach his son's heresies; a son can only pretend to worship his father's sacred cows. Inevitably the younger wins, for the future is with him. Even the Chinese, those notable admirers of their ancestors, have an adage which says: "What we call the spirit of the age, our fathers called the end of the world."[2]

Perhaps what we are experiencing in our generation is only another variation on this timeless theme. But one wonders if it does not go far deeper than usual. Is our alienation the most difficult kind of all, namely, that marked not by resistance but by indifference? The self-sufficiency that marks secularism easily becomes self-righteousness. Secularism has become an orthodoxy in our times, and it closes minds to the heresy of belief in anything transcendent. Whoever tries to address secularism with the biblical faith must inevitably have some pain of rejection.

The indifference is not new, by any means. Frederick W. Robertson felt it in his native Brighton, a seashore resort in England. In July, 1851, Robertson wrote these lines to a friend:

> I wish I did not hate preaching so much, but the degradation of being a Brighton preacher is almost intolerable. 'I cannot dig, to beg I am ashamed;' but I think there is not a hard-working artisan whose work does not seem to me a worthier and higher being than myself. I do not depreciate spiritual work—I hold it higher than secular; all I say and feel is, that by the change of times the pulpit has lost its place.[3]

This is a very personal matter. One does not do justice to preaching in our day without saying in all honesty that you search again and again for some access, however small, to the secular mind. It seems to have written off the gospel as irrelevant to its interest. If you care at all about persons, there's pain in confronting those described by Isaiah who

"Hear and hear, but do not understand;
see and see, but do not perceive."
—Isaiah 6:9

The Pain of Diversion

Consider, in the third place, *the pain of diversion.* For the gospel *does* get diverted, often in our time into structures, bureaucracies, and forms. I am not rejecting organized religion. After all, what is the alternative? Disorganized religion? But in our time, it seems to me, there is a very real danger that we walk straight into a kind of bureaucratic captivity. There comes a point at which we are serving our institutional forms more than we are serving the gospel. Those do not need to be alternatives, but they tend to become so.

There is an interesting response revealed in the story of the transfiguration (Luke 9:32-36). When the resplendent experience on the mountaintop had passed, revealing the significance of Jesus, it was Peter who made the first response, "'Master, it is well that we are here; let us make three booths, one for you and one for Moses and one for Elijah.'" Significantly the record adds, "not knowing what he said." That often is the first response to any great experience, "Let's build three booths," as though the experience could be captured by marking the spot. If that had happened, one can see persons down the ages taking care of those booths, hoping it all would happen again! The church constantly has to battle against the tendency to say, "Let's build a booth." Booth building is a major enterprise of all human endeavor in our time.

It needs to be clear what is being said here. This does not mean that the church does not *have* an institution. It couldn't get along without it. But, primarily, it is a great *family* of faith. We constantly have to monitor our structures to see that we are free to serve the gospel instead of the structure, to be an organism instead of an organization, and to be sure that the structures we build do not become the idols we serve.

Some of the most unhappy experiences in preaching, times when there is real pain in it, come when we try to serve the organization instead of the gospel. It is then that one has the uncomfortable feeling that the sermon might well be described by something William McAdoo said about the speeches of President Harding. He once recorded, "His speeches left the impression of an army of pompous phrases moving over

the landscape in search of an idea; sometimes these mean-
dering words would actually capture a straggling thought and
bear it triumphantly, a prisoner in their midst, until it died of
servitude and overwork."[4] That is what preaching easily becomes when we are diverted from the gospel to the institution.

The Pain of Absence

Now we must speak of the greatest pain of all. It is *the
pain of absence.* Paul's phrase has it, "Lest . . . when I have
preached to others, I myself should be a castaway" (1 Corinthians 9:27, KJV). But it does happen, and it happens to
all of us. We cannot suppose that ordination is inoculation.
It does not build immunity from the chills and fevers of faith
which all know. But God's absence is particularly painful for
ministers because we feel it *ought* not happen. It makes us
feel faithless; though if we listen to our biblical witness, we
soon find that it is only another side of faith.

In this we share the experience of our time. It's amazing
how obsessed our generation is with God, not with God's
presence but with God's absence! Our plays, our novels, our
biographies cannot let that experience alone. But it is interesting to note that absence is a form of knowledge. We never
know one is absent until we have first known that he or she
is present. We do not miss one whom we have not known;
there is no sense of absence about that. So we can take
comfort in the fact that as long as we know that God is absent
or distant, we still know God. It helps us see through the
sometimes agonizing crises of faith which are a part of our
calling.

Why does God seem absent from us at times? The question fits not only the church but also the human heart. Is it
to keep us from growing too glib, too stuffy, too certain about
the wrong things, that God sometimes is absent from us? No
one can say. But few of us could live long in the ministry
without asking the question. The pain of a crisis of faith for
the preacher is best described by the words of Aeschylus, "In
our sleep, pain which cannot forget falls drop by drop upon
the heart until, in our despair, against our will, comes wisdom
through the awful grace of God."[5]

These are some of the pains of preaching. For Paul this,
however, was only the preface to the full experience: "The
pain God is allowed to guide ends in a saving repentance

never to be regretted." That has a particular significance for preaching. For sometimes it is our pains that add the power in preaching. Robert Frost once described a poem in a way which is remarkably descriptive of a sermon. He said, "A poem is never a put-up job. . . . It begins as a lump in the throat, a sense of wrong, a homesickness, a lovesickness. It was never a thought to begin with. . . . It may be a big big emotion then and yet finds nothing it can embody in. It finds the thought and the thought finds the words."[6] That is a description of a sermon that has known pain.

When God guides that pain, it also guides our lives. The number of times when life is changed because we were convinced something was a good idea is comparatively small. But the number of times when it changed because the pain of *not* changing became unbearable is comparatively large.

It was the pain of preaching that started Karl Barth in the theological search to understand its meaning. It was the pain of his own sin that sent Luther to search for the meaning of salvation by faith. It was the pain of reconciling injustice with the meaning of the gospel that sent Walter Rauschenbusch to search for the wider meaning of redemption. It was the pain of his own failure that led John Wesley to search for the grace that would convert him. It was the pain of his own breakdown that caused Harry Emerson Fosdick to understand the power of faith to make people whole. We should be incomparably impoverished without the fruits of that experience: "The pain God is allowed to guide ends in a saving repentance never to be regretted." Strange as it may seem, it is the pain of preaching that becomes the power of preaching.

CHAPTER 6

What Do We Mean— Preach Christ?

The Book of Jonah, in which we often have become more fascinated by his means of transportation than his means of grace, has a revealing description of Jonah's experience. He had been commanded to go to Nineveh to preach, but he had set out in the opposite direction—to his disaster. Then the narrative says: "Then the word of the LORD came to Jonah the second time, saying, 'Arise, go to Nineveh . . .'" (Jonah 3:1-2). This time, taught by sobering experience, Jonah obeyed. He preached but one sermon and the whole city repented!

"The word of the LORD came to Jonah the second time." In fact, that seems to be a succinct statement of the nature of theological education itself. When we say that the Christian faith must be an examined faith, we are not questioning its truth, but we may be questioning whether we really were ready to hear the word when it came. We are not questioning what the faith is, but where we are! At no point is this more evident than in the necessity of thinking through repeatedly the message of the gospel.

Our purpose in this chapter is to turn that enquiry toward the central theme of the Christian faith, namely, to "preach Christ." That we are to preach Christ, none of us would question. In fact, that is the danger. It is a matter of such ready and universal agreement that it almost stops further thought. When we say that we "preach Christ," the phrase is so familiar that we easily assume we know the meaning of what we have said! If it is so central and so basic, is it not even more imperative that we examine what we are really saying? Does it mean the same thing in every generation? Or is it like the theme in a symphony, open to an amazing number of variations?

Particularly, can the New Testament meaning of the term be lifted bodily from the New Testament time to this? Do changes in the listeners require changes in the preaching? The question is not only theological, asking: Is it true? It is also homiletical, asking: Is it understood? These questions seem to impel, even compel, us to think things over again. What *do* we mean: Preach Christ?

Pursuing the answer to that question seems to set us on a path which runs through three considerations: First, what did the New Testament preachers mean when they spoke of preaching Christ? Second, if there were differences of emphasis, was there any consistent theme in them all, any central thrust that gave that word its nature and identity? And third, what, then, does it mean to preach Christ today?

New Testament Meanings

Our first consideration is to ask what the New Testament preachers meant when they preached Christ. The answer has to be found, of course, in those writings which reflect the life of the early church, namely, the book of Acts and the letters to the young churches. The theme we are examining emerged particularly in the preaching which sought to interpret the faith to both Jew and Gentile. That the purpose, in season and out, was to "preach Christ" seems clear beyond dispute. Yet there were variations in the proclamation which seem significant.

It should be noted in passing what it clearly did *not* mean. To "preach Christ" was not simply the attempt to present the facts about his earthly life. It was not to deal with those facts which interest a biographer: where he was born, where he lived, even for the most part, what he taught. It made no attempt to deal with the principles by which he lived, or the persons to whom he related. It was not *facts* about Jesus which they preached. It was *faith* about him. It dealt not so much with occurrence as with significance. They were proclaiming not biography, but theology. They seemed to count irrelevant the normal journalistic questions: Who? Where? What? They dealt mostly with "why?" That theme comes out with at least four variations.

1. Often it meant preaching *Christ as the Messiah.* The book of Acts makes this clear again and again. In chapter 5, it is recorded, "And every day in the temple and at home they did not cease teaching and preaching Jesus as the Christ" (5:42). Again, in chapter 17, "'This Jesus, whom I proclaim to you, is the Christ'" (v. 3).

In saying this, of course, they were relating Jesus to the deepest level of faith for the hearers. The hope for the Messiah was so deep-rooted that it must have seemed inborn. From earliest childhood they had heard of that hope. In the many times of darkness, for the Jews it was the hope of the Messiah which sustained them. The promise of what the Messiah would bring was the brightest of their hopes. Their very identity as a people was affirmed by the belief that the Messiah was coming *for them.* Every delay only increased their awareness of how good it would be when the Messiah came.

It is impossible for us who have not been brought up in that centuries-old hope to know how deep it ran. It was the mainstream in their common life. So when the Christian message was that "he has come at last," it went to the very heart of the matter. They knew what they were accepting or rejecting. No one had to explain who the Messiah was. They only had to decide whether this Jesus was indeed he. So to preach Christ as the Messiah was emotionally charged in either the acceptance or the rejection of that word.

2. It is evident that they *preached him as Savior.* Often that Saviorhood was in the present time, the saving work now centering in the death and resurrection from which came for us all the power that brings us into new life. That was Paul's word to the Corinthians: "We preach Christ crucified, a stumbling block to Jews and folly to Gentiles, but to those who are called, both Jews and Greeks, Christ the power of God and the wisdom of God" (1 Corinthians 1:23-24). There seems little doubt that preaching the resurrection and its power was very close to the heart of "preaching Christ,"

But sometimes the meaning of Jesus as Savior was a *future* hope finding residence in the belief that he would come again. It was to the Philippians that Paul said, "For our citizenship is in heaven, from which also we eagerly wait for a

Savior, the Lord Jesus Christ" (Philippians 3:20, *New American Standard Bible*). But present or future, Christ as Savior was a theme of the New Testament preaching, as of ours.

3. It is further evident that those early Christians *preached Jesus Christ as Lord*. This theme is stated unforgettably, of course, in Second Corinthians, "For what we preach is not ourselves, but Jesus Christ as Lord, with ourselves as your servants for Jesus' sake" (4:5). The term "Lord" seems to have conveyed several important meanings. It always connoted a *living* Lord, thus recognizing the wonder of his ongoing life after the resurrection. It affirmed Christ as Lord of the church, making clear that life in the congregation was life under Christ, and in him. Probably few words are more inclusive and descriptive of what it meant to "preach Christ." They were saying most of the things important to their faith when they preached him as Lord.

4. It is clear that *preaching Christ meant proclaiming the coming of the kingdom*. In this, of course, they picked up the theme of Jesus himself, that "the kingdom is at hand." For the early church Jesus himself became the sign of that kingdom, himself the evidence of what he had proclaimed. Moreover, the healing ministry and other signs often were interpreted as evidence of the inbreaking kingdom. So in chapter 8 of Acts, we read of Philip going into Samaria to preach. His ministry of healing was the prelude to his preaching. ". . . they believed Philip as he preached good news about the kingdom of God and the name of Jesus Christ . . ." (v. 12).

Even so cursory a survey reveals two things about the meaning of preaching Christ as practiced in the primitive church: First, that it had several meanings, not one. It was inclusive, not exclusive—not insisting on a single meaning. All of these meanings, to be sure, affirmed Christ as central and regnant. But the significance of his centrality was interpreted in several ways.

There is evidence that sometimes these meanings became competitive, even controversial. Those controversies are convincingly documented in the letters of Paul. The Apostle is even explicit about that in the letter to the Philippians: "Some indeed preach Christ from envy and rivalry . . . [and] proclaim Christ out of partisanship . . ." (1:15-17). This is no surprise to anyone who has lived in the life of the church! The surprise, if any, is how early in the history of the church it began.

The second truth which impresses us in reviewing the New Testament record is that the terms used to convey the meaning of Christ *were a part of the language before Christ came.* The terms we have noted, Messiah, Savior, Lord, kingdom, were deep within the culture, the honored and cherished words of faith. Preaching Christ did not create those words; it simply claimed them. It went to deep places in the life of faith and related Jesus Christ to them. It preached Christ as fulfillment, the coming of one who long has been anticipated and who, in his coming, fulfilled the hopes and needs as understood in that generation. It could be said, then, that preaching Christ is most succinctly summed up in Paul's statement in another context to the Corinthians, "For all the promises of God find their Yes in him" (2 Corinthians 1:20).

The Underlying Theme

Our inquiry now comes to focus on a single question. If there are, indeed, several aspects in which Christ was preached, is there any underlying theme which gives them all a continuity and identity? What runs through them all, by the presence of which we know that this, indeed, is preaching Christ? It seems to me that there are three marks of that essence for which we are searching.

The first mark is the word that "God was in Christ." Jesus is God, acting. It was God's initiative that set the world into motion; God's purpose that determines the end toward which it is moving; God's nature that is disclosed; God who, in Christ, "might illuminate the world by His wisdom and excite it to the love of Himself,"[1] as Abélard put it. That is the ground which all the special emphases have in common, whether one speaks of Messiah or Savior or Lord or kingdom. "God was in Christ."

The second mark is the word that, in Christ, God has come, reconciling "the world to himself" (2 Corinthians 5:19). In Christ, God addresses the real *world*, not the abstraction, not the idea, but the throbbing, hating, vibrant, colorful, longing world of human experience. Preaching Christ is not like fourth-class mail, "to whom it may concern." It is personal, with our names on it.

The third mark is the radical word which marks a discontinuity with what we have been. Preaching Christ does not call for something merely added; it is a new beginning. Christ becomes the first fact which all else must acknowledge. The words are those of conception and birth. A new life has begun. "If any one is in Christ, he is a new creation" (2 Corinthians 5:17). It is not *more* life; it is *other* life. The difference is qualitative.

Two Observations

Now we are under the necessity of moving on to that which has been our primary concern from the beginning, namely, what it means to preach Christ in our generation. If these themes are constant, what do they mean in terms of our time? Reinhold Neibuhr has noted that there are those who "regard Christ 'as foolishness' because they have no questions for which Christ is the answer. . . ."[2] We certainly are asking questions these days, and they are not questions for idle discussion, but they are the questions of our survival. If, as we have seen, the New Testament preacher proclaimed Christ, addressed to the hungers and needs of that time, can we not preach him addressed to the needs of our time?

Before confronting that question more precisely, we need to modify it with two observations. First, while each generation has its distinctive questions, most questions of human existence do remain the same, whatever the culture or time. In these forty years in the pulpit I have been made aware, again and again, that the questions to which the gospel must be addressed remain the timeless basic questions of human life. The people in our congregation would have much in common with the congregations of the primitive church and the Reformation church in Holland and England. In every generation we need the good tidings of God's presence as a "very present help in time of trouble." We need to know that we are loved and that we can love. We need assurance to face the anxieties which beset us. We need to hear the good news of our worth in God's eyes and in the eyes of a loving community, thus speaking to the personal struggle to maintain self-esteem. We need forgiveness for our sins and hope for our endeavors, and we need to hear the faith that can transcend death. There is no generation in which these are not true.

The second modification is that our faith has its own language, and we still can rejoice in the words of the New

Testament generations. They have become the household words of our faith. Like any family we have words that belong only to us. Messiah and Savior are not the words we grew up with in our culture, but they are the words that we grew into in our family of faith, and we have a love for them. In our hymns and our Scripture they become the *faith language* of every generation, providing a continuity that turns our history into our biography.

But having said this, I am persuaded that each generation also has its own questions, and I believe that to preach Christ is also to address those questions with the truth that is in him. That's not only the *duty* of preaching. That's also the *excitement* of it. It means that one part of preaching is, as T. S. Eliot put it, "to apprehend the point of intersection of the timeless with time."[3]

Contemporary Openings

So once again we ask: What does it mean to preach Christ today? When we have taken into account the continuity of human experience and the validity of faith language, there still is an imperative upon us to address the particularities of our time. We will consider four contemporary areas where preaching Christ takes on particular meaning. There are four hungers evident in our time to which we believe the Good News of Christ can and must be addressed.

The first is the hunger for *liberation*. Howard Thurman relates that years ago, when he was a guest preacher in India, he was in his room late at night when he heard a tapping at the door. When he opened it, a young Indian boy stood timidly before him. As though he had been working up courage for this moment of meeting, he exclaimed immediately, "I stood outside the window tonight and heard you speak. Tell me, have you got any hope for a nobody?" Then his courage gave out, and he dashed off into the bushes without waiting for an answer.[4] But in the subsequent years that question has been heard around the world in all circumstances: "Have you got any hope for a nobody?" It is evident that it will not be silenced. One way or another, this generation will turn where persons believe the answer is to be found.

It seems almost inevitable that there should emerge, therefore, in our time, what has been called "liberation theology." Disinherited men and women, some of them desperate and determined, have felt that Jesus identified with them. Again, as Thurman put it, the Good News is for those whose backs are to the wall.[5] They hear Jesus at Nazareth again, preaching good news to the poor, proclaiming release to the captives and liberty for those who are oppressed.

The emergence of liberation theology seems, to me, a faithful response to our time, the evidence that Christ's work has not ceased upon the earth, the reminder that Christ is born anew in each generation, as an infant, to live that generation's life with them.

That liberation, while urgently political and economic in many ways, is not confined to these areas. There are oppressions of the spirit of which a secular generation is becoming acutely aware. We may not use the words as often as other generations, but we are still bound by sin and unfaith and meaninglessness and fear. It seems that the time of judgment is upon our secular day and untold numbers cry within themselves, "O wretched man that I am! who shall deliver me from the body of this death?" (Romans 7:24, KJV). If we preach Christ as liberator, we will speak to this time.

Second, there is the hunger for *humanness*. It is not necessary to repeat here the oft-told story of depersonalization which increasingly marks our cultures. Numbers take the place of names. More importantly, depersonalization becomes dehumanization. It is not surprising that there has come a deep-laid hunger to be a "human being" or, as it is often stated, to be "fully human." In our century this often leads people into superficial programs which promise self-improvement or "getting in touch with yourself." Recent youth movements, seeming to be rebellion against oppressive structures, prove, on closer examination, to be basically a hope to get out from under dehumanizing forces.

Can we preach Christ to that hunger? Decidedly yes. We sometimes forget that the great struggle of the early church creeds was to preserve Jesus' *humanity*. The fight was to keep him really identified with human experience and our earthly common life, while affirming his deity which seemed so manifest to the emerging church. So the Council of Chalcedon which, in the eyes of many, has remained as the definitive statement of Christian creedal confession said, "We all with one consent teach men to confess one and the same Son, our Lord Jesus Christ, the same perfect in Godhead and the same perfect in manhood, truly God and the same truly man."

What this affirms is audacious in two regards: one, that in Jesus God drew near, but the other, that in him the full meaning of humanity is revealed. In Jesus we see not only God, but we also see a person—what we were meant to be and what we can be. The Jerusalem Conference of 1925 stated even more simply, "In Christ we know who God is and what through Him man may become." The fruit of the gospel is persons fully alive. If *that* is the aspect of preaching which reaches out to this generation, then we should preach it, knowing that we are, indeed, in the mainstream of Christian thought.

In July, 1835, Kierkegaard had a hilltop experience in which the conflicting factors in his life "joined hands and became friends." Of that moment his biographer says, "He came down from that hilltop in possession of his own personality, as never before."[6] In countless ways, men and women reveal their hunger for that experience. If Jesus, in whom humanity was fulfilled, can be preached to *that* hunger, we will speak to our time.

There is a third hunger which marks us. It is the hunger for *hope*. We are thinking here of the *social* hope. No century began with higher hopes for human societies. The vision was abroad of a world which would bring war under control, achieve a high measure of justice for oppressed peoples, and make significant inroads on poverty. Yet we, the second and third generations of that century, have seen the world seemingly go in the opposite direction, until today serious and concerned people wonder if we are to survive. Science, the hope at the beginning of the century, has become the prophet of despair as the final quarter begins. Great numbers of people would confess with one of our American poets,

> One by one, like leaves from a tree
> All my faiths have forsaken me.[7]

Can we preach Christ as social hope? We must weigh that carefully. Jesus did not, to any degree, deal with the morality of nations or the ethics of social bodies. He did speak of a kingdom of righteousness, and he was sure that the kingdom of God would prevail. He moved in the prophetic strain which assumed and proclaimed the sovereignty of God and, especially, a concern for the nation of Israel. We do not have a blueprint, but we do have a covenant. We may not be sure of the *way,* but the *will* of God is manifest in him. We can trust that "somehow good will be the final goal of ill"[8] and that "Though the wrong seems oft so strong, God is the Ruler yet"! To preach Jesus Christ as that assurance is to provide hope for the soul in a time when we are threatened with being swept away on a tidal wave of despair.

Finally, there seems, indeed, to be a hunger for *joy.* Even our search for a "good time," sometimes grown desperate, can be a flight from a joyless life. Most people feel that life is meant to have joy in it. Yet it seems that few find it. On a napkin, on a bar, were found these words, in which someone sensed the nature of that "good time":

> Faces along the bar
> Cling to their average day;
> The lights must never go out,
> The music must always play.
> Lest we should see where we are,
> Lost in a haunted wood,
> Children afraid of the night
> Who have never been happy or good.

This is a generation which needs to learn the distinction between merely having a good time and experiencing joy. Jesus drew that contrast in the story of the prodigal son. He made clear that, when the son first started out in search for a life of his own, he "wasted his substance in riotous living" (Luke 15:13, KJV). Generally speaking, many in our generation equate that with having a good time, even with a form of joyous living. But it soon ended in loneliness and loss. The story has a revealing phrase at the end. After the restoration of the broken relationships, and after the son had found himself again, "they began to be merry" (15:24, KJV). What a different kind of good time this was! We sense the spontaneity, the lightheartedness, the celebration. All was well at last.

Making Christ Known

But the time for analysis is past. We have, indeed, carried out the necessity of thinking through the message of the gospel. It is my hope that the Son of man indeed has come to us again.

But when all is said and done, the overarching truth about preaching Christ is the privilege of it. Yes, and the wonder. What an inexhaustible subject it is, fresh with every generation. One cannot think of any calling more demanding, more exciting, and more marked by privilege.

At the last, then, the words of G. A. Johnston Ross seem our testimony, too: "'By "preaching Christ" I mean no less and no more than working to make Christ known and welcomed and beloved and adored and followed and trusted by one's fellow men.'"9

CHAPTER 7

The Christian Hope—
Foolish but Not Futile

On a bright Sunday morning in June, in a village church in upstate New York, I was ordained to the Christian ministry. The economic depression was heavy upon us, but our spirits were light. My memory is not only of the happening, but of the feeling. My father was up from Ohio to preach the sermon. By the fortunate circumstances of an annual meeting of the American Baptist Convention in Rochester, an impressive number of those who had shared in the formation of my life were present. The mood of the day could only be expressed by a line from Washington Gladden's hymn, "In hope that sends a shining ray far down the future's broad'ning way" ("O Master, Let Me Walk with Thee").

In fact, we had written a hymn of hope for that occasion. Looking back I can see that it was a distinguished hymn— distinguished, that is, by its sexist language and its humanist views! To a theme from Brahms' First Symphony we marched in, singing:

> Ye sons of the Father,
> Who follow the vision fair,
> Come, light at His altar
> The torch which your strong arms bear.
> For men long for freedom,
> Justice and mercy,
> Hope for a better day.
> O come, at His call,
> We shall offer our all,
> And bring in the Kingdom fair.

So if there was a depression—as there certainly was—it was not in our expectations. We were full of belief and genuinely expected to bring in that "kingdom fair," or at least one more fair than it ever had been before!

Well, how has it gone? How fares the vision fair after four decades? In a mere turning of a thought, the mind does an instant replay. Four years after that processional, World War II began. Later we learned that, at the very time the hymn was written, there was going on in Europe a holocaust of unprecedented proportions, the incredible genocide of six million Jews.

From that time the story unfolds with an unhalting procession of names that tell our history: Hiroshima, Korea, Vietnam. At home there were names, too: Watts, Birmingham, Detroit, Rochester. Then there were the fallen: John Kennedy, Robert Kennedy, Martin Luther King, Jr.

To be sure, at home a procession of alphabet programs had appeared, but almost every daily paper brought disclosure of corruption and the abuse of our best social plans. Abroad, in this century, one-half of the world's people have undergone revolution, one-third of them since World War II. But in the main those revolutions have not brought forth free societies, as we might have imagined or hoped, but new forms of controlled society. Put all this together and one has to say in all honesty that the evil has been so much worse than we could have imagined.

Perhaps a kind of ultimate has been reached in the words of Richard Falk, who predicts the future in terms of decades. The 1970s, he said, would be characterized by the politics of despair; the 1980s by a politics of desperation; the 1990s by the politics of catastrophe, and the twenty-first century will be the era of annihilation. [1]

In more measured words, Robert H. Heilbroner, in a book entitled *An Inquiry into the Human Prospect,* sums it up by saying, "If then, by the question 'Is there hope for man?' we ask whether it is possible to meet the challenges of the future without the payment of a fearful price, the answer must be: No, there is no such hope." [2]

In his classic, *Moby Dick,* Herman Melville has a scene in which the men in a small whaling boat are tossed overboard by an overwhelming wave. They manage to scramble back into the boat which is half filled with water and so wait for rescue by the mother ship. One of them, Starbuck, discovers a waterproof match keg and is able to light a tiny lantern. This he fastens to the end of an oar and, placing himself into the prow of the boat, sits holding it aloft in the darkness. Of this scene Melville says, "There, then, he sat, holding up that imbecile candle in the heart of that almighty forlornness. There, then, he sat, the sign and symbol of a man without faith, hopelessly holding up hope in the midst of despair."[3]

In a way in which our secular culture could not have foreseen, the biblical faith begins increasingly to stand out as the only light in the midst of our "almighty forlornness." What is the ground of that hope? How can it stand in such a time? By every standard my generation ought to be in despair. But as a professing Christian I want to make clear that I am not in despair. Rather, this is a time to hold up a hope which seems foolish to many, even an imbecile candle in the heart of our almighty forlornness.

For some of us, new meaning has come into an ancient hope. There was a time when we thought that sociology or psychology or a theology which believed in human progress would carry us through. And now we have come to discover that the hope is where we least expected to find it, namely, in the eschatology of the Christian gospel. Yes, that's right— the eschatology. There was a time when those who had social concern thought that was part of the earthen vessel that held the treasure. It was the hope of a biblical day, not ours. We are coming to discover that it is, in fact, part of the treasure, for it is an affirmation of the ultimate assured victory of God in human life.

In our century we have seen several basic Christian doctrines radically challenged. In the first third of this century the question of God as Creator seemed challenged by the expanding universe. Later, there came the questions about the Christian doctrine of humankind, in the light of some developments in psychology, particularly the Freudian, and in the light of those totalitarian movements which would submerge man to the state. We have seen our way fairly well through those crises. Now another is upon us. It centers not upon the doctrine of God as Creator, or the Christian doctrine of humankind, but upon the belief that God is the Lord of history.

Can we really preach that? In the light of what we have known, experienced, and seen, in the light of our steady defeats, and our delayed victories, can we preach that? Many of the things we thought would happen did not happen, and many we thought couldn't, *have* happened. Yet today I want to bear witness that many in my generation are not in despair. To the contrary, we have come into a kind of heady hope which no longer rests upon the evidences that a secular day can bring forth. What is that hope? It rests where the biblical hope must rest, namely, in the nature and word of God as it has been disclosed to us.

It may be helpful to speak of that hope in two regards: first, the immanent, and second, the ultimate.

The Immanent Hope

First, consider that *immanent hope which is ours in the biblical faith*. The immanent victories are never complete, but they are not totally delayed either. God reveals divine victories even in the processes of life. There seem to be "built-in" victories that support our belief that God indeed is Lord of history—not only distant history, but today's events.

This raises a basic question: What in the world is God doing now? One can answer that only by faith, but it is a faith which I believe we have every right to claim. For God is doing something in this world and I, for one, believe that we can trust it.

First, I believe that *God is judging.* Are social and historical processes as morally indifferent as it sometimes seems? That great preacher and courageous Christian, Ernest Tittle, once confessed that, as a chaplain in World War I, he came out of a field hospital overwhelmed by the carnage he saw and stood in the trench, pounding on the ground and saying, "Where's God? Why doesn't He do something?"[4] None of us is alien to that feeling. *Is* God doing something?

Before World War I Benito Mussolini was a devotee of freedom. He even wrote a book on the life of John Huss. But in later years he became a tyrant himself and his life ended with his body hanging by the heels in a square in Milan. His first truth that believed in freedom was more powerful than he knew.

To be sure, it rarely is that dramatic. But is the fact of judgment any less true? Of many an evil, it can be said: This will self-destruct. Santayana once observed that evil perishes of its own excess. The judgment of God is not only in intervention but also in inner working. Some of the most far-reaching judgments are silent and even unseen. The deception of advertising means no one believes anyone after a while; the pursuit of power takes on an increasingly desperate pace, increasing anxiety, decreasing certainty; privilege without justice produces its own decadence. The silent judgments are starkly real.

Watch a child running downhill. When the child first starts down, feeling the pull of gravity, it's a heady kind of freedom, a surge of power. But watch. There comes a point where the same gravity that sets the child free begins to take over. Freedom gives way to fear, then to panic, and unless a saving hand intervenes, the end of it is a fall. Every day we learn the meaning of that kind of judgment.

Again, I believe *God is conserving.* As the physical world has the conservation of energy, the world of spirit seems to have the conservation of concern. I believe it is God at work.

That faith emerges in Dietrich Bonhoeffer's letters from prison. On September 23, 1943, he ended a letter to his parents with these words:

> On reading this letter through, I think it sounds a bit disgruntled. That is not what I intend, and it wouldn't represent my state of mind. Much as I long to be out of here, I don't believe a single day has been wasted. What will come out of my time here it's still too early to say; but something will come of it.[5]

Something will come of it, indeed! There was a day on a plane when I was reading the little red paperback of his letters, and the stewardess stopped and said, "I see you are reading Bonhoeffer." "I certainly am," I said, "but where did you learn about him?" "Oh," she said, "our chaplain at Wooster College talked about him all the time. I read him a lot." There was that dinner in our home when we were welcoming friends on leave from Zaire in Africa. They had barely arrived in Africa before the students in theological school, learning that one of the doctors had come from East Germany, said, "Tell us about Dietrich." Bonhoeffer was right, "It will not be wasted." God was doing a new thing in him.

Some faith like that has to undergird our preaching, doesn't it? We are really hard pressed to get our results into any annual report, no matter how much we are urged to get it all on the record. It's that kind of faith which enables us, at times, to hear the word given to a Scot preacher one day. He came to church full of the assurance that he had one of the greatest sermons ever preached. So, proud of it, he mounted the high pulpit, only to have the experience all of us know so well: his words were hollow and lifeless. So, humiliated, he came down. At the base of the steps he was met by a little woman who took him by the hand and said, "Ah, laddie, if ye had gone up the way ye came down, ye might have come down the way ye went up." Well, let it be our faith that it may be so! It will not be wasted.

Once more, God is not only judging and conserving, as we believe. *God also is surprising us.* Surprises are part of God's mighty acts.

What surprises there are! We are such planners! We decide how God must come into human affairs. We treat it all with a kind of public relations twist. We pick the time and the place. We insure that the right people are there to meet God. We get the news releases out as to what to expect. We even have some prepared quotes. But God has an uncanny way of taking care of the times and places and entrances. While we wait at the airport, as it were, with a representative committee of dignitaries and an escort, waiting for the coming, God has a way of quietly arriving at the bus station, walking up a side street, and slipping, unnoticed, through the servant's entrance. When we find out, at last, that God is here, we wonder, as they wondered in Jesus' time, "Can any good thing come out of Nazareth?"

That's something we have forgotten in our times of despair. Who can say what surprises already are taking place? From what Nazareth do you suppose Christ will come in our time? The surprises are so many. Pope John was a surprise. In a decade the Catholic Church opened doors which, in other eras, would have taken at least a century. Dag Hammarskjöld was a surprise. Who could have supposed that a man of mystic faith sat at the council tables where the tensions of our world are most felt? Rosa Parks was a surprise, calling out all that courage and resistance at the moment when it was needed. Only God knows when any time has come to "kairos." The ancient historian Herodotus said that history itself is the recording of surprises. Rauschenbusch said it another way: "History never moves as men intend. . . . We hoist the sails but another holds the helm."[6] Has God run out of surprises in our time? Has it at last gone beyond God? Or do we live

through our threatening despair by expecting someone or
something to come out of the Nazareth God will choose in
our time?

So the immanent acts of God are in divine judging, conserving, and surprising. But one thing more. To see the community of believers is to know that God also is *gathering*,
calling out a new community. The kingdom is not only future.
It is already among us. It is now and we are living in it.

During the war a young man was brought for hearing
before a magistrate because of his pacifist position. The judge
listened, not unsympathetically, then said, "But, son, you are
trying to live in the kingdom of God. And the kingdom has
not come yet." To which the other replied. "It has come for
me, and I can't go on living as though it has not!"

We easily are aware of the things that are dying in our
time. They are many and they are far-reaching. But new things
are being born. One is the new community which has been
emerging ever since Christ came. From the time those first
Christians, touched by him, proclaimed a new nation in which
there is neither Jew nor Greek, bond nor free, male nor fe-
male, it has been here. There has been a new nation of those
who are "in Christ." It transcends all else. It often leaves us
aliens and pilgrims in everyday life. But it is here and it cannot
be put off. Christ opened that new nation to us, and no one
can close that door. In it we take a new name. We become a
new family. In it we say "brother" and "sister," and these are
not future. These are now.

That's why Christians are so scandalously given to joy—
in spite of the very real griefs and defeats. Often we come
out with an illogical joy, because we celebrate what is, in spite
of all the denials of life. Do you remember Chanticleer, Ro-
stand's rooster, who believed that his crowing brought the
dawn? It seemed true, too, for every morning he crowed, and
the sun came over the horizon as though in response to his
beckoning. But one day came the moment of truth. A hen-
pheasant, jealous of the dawn, covered his eyes and the dawn
came anyway, without his crowing. Chanticleer had an identity
crisis. But he came through. Even if his crowing did not bring
the dawn, he was confident that his call might be of comfort
on a gray morning.[7] He would celebrate the dawn.

Perhaps the new note of celebration in our faith these
days is the discovering that when we face our powerlessness,

we find the greater power beyond us. And if the new day is not so much our achievement, as we had supposed, as it is God's gift, is it any less a cause of celebration? Or is it more? That's why Christians like Paul and Silas can sing even when in prison at midnight! God invites us *now* into his kingdom and we say yes! Thus he gathers his new community of faith.

The Ultimate Hope

These are immanent victories and we shall expect them. But it remains for us to speak of the hope in God's *ultimate* victory. While we may not feel at home in the eschatological context of the New Testament, we certainly can reaffirm our faith in its basic affirmation. In God's own time and own way, God *will* prevail. And so we sing, "Though the wrong seems oft so strong, God is the Ruler yet!" Unproved, but unmoved, that faith is the anchorage for a time like this.

Perhaps the word of God for our generation is the one spoken to Joshua, the successor to Moses. As Moses had led the people through the wilderness to stand at the border of Canaan, the Promised Land, so Joshua's responsibility was to take the people in to possess it. Following the fall of Jericho, Joshua decided to move on the town of Ai. He sent out people to spy out the land and they came back with a report which was to prove disastrous. They said, "There's no need to send all the people into Ai. Two or three thousand will do it." So Joshua took this intelligence report at its face value and acted upon it. The results were a humiliating defeat. The men of Ai met the Israelites on the heights and drove them back, killing some of their number. And the record says, "The hearts of the people melted, and became as water" (Joshua 7:5).

At this humiliation and defeat, Joshua fell on his face, tore his clothing, threw dust on his head, and cried out loud. Then it was that the word of the Lord came to Joshua. The Lord said, ". . . why have you thus fallen upon your face? . . . Up . . . and say, 'Sanctify yourselves for tomorrow'" (Joshua 7:10, 13).

Only the Christian pulpit has the ground for that word. "Why have you fallen thus on your face? Up . . . and say, 'Sanctify yourselves for tomorrow.'"

That ordination processional, to which I referred earlier, was a long time ago—so long ago that one day, sooner than I would choose, it will be time for the recessional. What will be the closing hymn of a ministry in our century, in the light of all our pain and frustration? What would it be? Certainly, no longer the glib, "Ye sons of the Father, come light at His altar the torch which your strong arms bear." No, not that. Rather, with a kind of unexplained confidence and unexamined serenity, one would choose for the recessional time of a ministry a great hymn:

How firm a foundation
Ye saints of the Lord,
Is laid for your faith in his excellent word!

. . . . . .

For I will be near thee, thy troubles to bless
And sanctify to thee thy deepest distress.

. . . . . .

"That soul, though all hell should endeavor to shake
I'll never, no never, no never forsake!"
—George Keith, "How Firm a Foundation"

Notes

Introduction

[1] William Wordsworth, "Prelude," section XI, line 303, *Major British Writers* (New York: Harcourt Brace Jovanovich, Inc., 1959), p. 75.

[2] Floyd Shacklock, *This Revolutionary Faith* (New York: Friendship Press, 1955), chapter 2.

[3] John Fowles, *The French Lieutenant's Woman* (Boston: Little, Brown & Company, 1969), p. 480.

Chapter 1

[1] Karl Barth, *The Word of God and the Word of Man* (New York: Harper & Row, Publishers, Inc., 1928), p. 125.

[2] Eberhard Busch, *Karl Barth*, trans. John Bowden (Philadelphia: Fortress Press, 1976), p. 101.

[3] Phillips Brooks, "The New and Greater Miracle" in *The Light of the World and Other Sermons* (New York: E. P. Dutton & Company, 1910), p. 34.

[4] Grace Noll Crowell, *Poems of Inspiration and Courage* (New York: Harper & Row, Publishers, Inc., 1965), p. 210. Copyright 1936 by Harper & Row, Publishers, Inc., renewed 1964 by Grace Noll Crowell. Reprinted by permission of the publisher.

[5] See Erik H. Erikson, "Identity and the Life Cycle," *Psychological Issues*, vol. 1, no. 1 (1959).

[6] Thomas M. Lindsay, *A History of the Reformation* (New York: Charles Scribner's Sons, 1906), vol. 1, p. 290.

[7] Thornton Wilder, *The Eighth Day* (New York: Harper & Row, Publishers, Inc., 1967), pp. 248-250.

Chapter 2

[1]John Dos Passos, *The Men Who Made the Nation* (Garden City, N. Y.: Doubleday & Co., Inc., 1957), p. 135.

[2]John Paterson, *The Goodly Fellowship of the Prophets* (New York: Charles Scribner's Sons, 1948), p. vii.

[3]James Muilenburg, *The Way of Israel* (New York: Harper & Row, Publishers, Inc., 1961), pp. 74-93.

[4]Paul Tillich, *The Eternal Now* (New York: Charles Scribner's Sons, 1963), p. 100.

[5]Joseph Wood Krutch, "If I May Say So," in *The American Scholar,* vol. 32 (Winter, 1963), p. 18.

[6]Jean Anouilh, *Becket* (New York: Coward-McCann, Inc., 1960), p. 112. Copyright 1960 Coward-McCann, Inc.; used by permission of Coward, McCann & Geoghegan, Inc.

Chapter 3

[1]Karl Barth, *The Word of God and the Word of Man* (New York: Harper & Row, Publishers, Inc., 1957), pp. 122-123.

[2]P. T. Forsyth, *Positive Preaching and the Modern Mind* (New York: Armstrong & Son, 1907), p. 3.

[3]Georgia Harkness, *John Calvin: The Man and His Ethics* (Nashville: Abingdon Press, 1958), p. 18.

[4]John Robinson, quoted in Harry Emerson Fosdick, *Great Voices of the Reformation* (New York: Random House, Inc., 1952), p. 546.

[5]Phillips Brooks, *Lectures on Preaching* (New York: E. P. Dutton & Company, 1878), p. 8.

[6]Emil Brunner, *The Divine–Human Encounter,* trans. Amandus W. Loos (Philadelphia: The Westminster Press, 1943).

[7]Samuel Valentine Cole, *Monica: The Chronicle of Marcus* (Boston: Marshall Jones Co., 1926), pp. 51-52.

Chapter 4

[1]Herman Melville, *Moby Dick,* Great Books of the Western World (Chicago: University of Chicago Press, 1952), pp. 29-30.

[2]*Ibid.*

[3]Alan Richardson, *Christian Apologetics* (New York: Harper & Row, Publishers, Inc., 1947), p.51.

[4]John Robinson, quoted in Harry Emerson Fosdick, *Great Voices of the Reformation* (New York: Random House, Inc., 1952), p. 546.

[5]Reinhold Niebuhr, *The Nature and Destiny of Man,* vol. 2 (New York: Charles Scribner's Sons, 1947), p. 6.

[6]Eberhard Busch, *Karl Barth,* trans. John Bowden (Philadelphia: Fortress Press, 1976), p.472.

Chapter 5

[1]Phillips Brooks, *The Purpose and Use of Comfort* (New York: E. P. Dutton & Company, 1910), p. 20.

[2]Alan Valentine, *Fathers to Sons* (Norman, Okla.: University of Oklahoma Press, 1963), p. xx.

[3]Stopford A. Brooke, *Life and Letters of Rev. F. W. Robertson*, vol. II (London: Kegan Paul, Trench, Trubner & Co., Ltd., 1907), p. 54.

[4]Mark Sullivan, *Our Times*, vol. 6, The Twenties (New York: Charles Scribner's Sons, 1926), p. 31.

[5]Quoted in Arthur Schlesinger, Jr., *Violence: America in the Sixties* (New York: The New American Library, Inc., 1968), p. 95.

[6]*Letters of Robert Frost to Louis Untermeyer* (New York: Holt, Rinehart, & Winston, 1963), p.22.

Chapter 6

[1]Victor Gollancz, *Man and God* (Boston: Houghton Mifflin Company, 1951), p. 45.

[2]Reinhold Niebuhr, *The Nature and Destiny of Man*, vol. 2 (New York: Charles Scribner's Sons, 1947), p. 6.

[3]T. S. Eliot, *Complete Poems and Plays* (New York: Harcourt Brace Jovanovich, Inc., 1952), p. 136.

[4]Howard Thurman, *Jesus and the Disinherited* (Nashville: Abingdon Press, 1949), p. 13.

[5]*Ibid.*, p. 14.

[6]E. L. Allen, *Kierkegaard—His Life and Thought* (New York: Harper & Row, Publishers, Inc., 1935), p. 11.

[7]Sara Teasdale, "Leaves," in *Collected Poems of Sara Teasdale* (New York: Macmillan Publishing Co., 1915). Reprinted with permission of Macmillan Publishing Co., Inc., from *Collected Poems of Sara Teasdale*, copyright 1915 by Macmillan Publishing Co., Inc., renewed 1943 by Mamie T. Wheliss.

[8]Alfred, Lord Tennyson, "In Memoriam," *The Home Book of Verse* (New York: Henry Holt and Company, 1945), p. 2900.

[9]Rolland W. Schloerb, *The Preaching Ministry Today* (New York: Harper & Row, Publishers, Inc., 1946), p. 3.

Chapter 7

[1]Cited in Robert L. Heilbroner, *An Inquiry into the Human Prospect* (New York: W. W. Norton & Company, Inc., 1974), p. 44.

[2]*Ibid.*, p. 136.

[3]Herman Melville, *Moby Dick*, Great Books of the Western World (Chicago: University of Chicago Press, 1952), p. 197.

[4]From a lecture given at Colgate Rochester Divinity School, May, 1942.

[5]Dietrich Bonhoeffer, *Letters and Papers from Prison*, paperback edition (New York: Macmillan, Inc., 1972), p. 114.

[6]Dores Robinson Sharpe, *Walter Rauschenbusch* (New York: Macmillan, Inc., 1942), p. 187.

[7]William Rose Benet, *The Reader's Encyclopedia*, vol. 1 (New York: Thomas Y. Crowell Company, Publishers, 1965), p. 196.